# MASTERING STM32 IOT PROJECTS

## A Hands-on Guide for STM32 to Build Secure and Scalable IoT Solutions

By

Janani Selvam

# TABLE OF CONTENTS

# WRITE THE I2C-LCD LIBRARY

Whoever wants to understand the library irrespective of what MCU you are using. This is the eye to see LCD library source file that we are going to discuss today. Before we jump into it, let's see the connection one more time. This is how the PCF 8574 is connected with the LCD, and as you can see, it only requires two wires to be connected to the MCU. Here I am showing the connection with the STM 32, but it remains the same for whatever MCU you are using. All you need to do is connect the clock pin to the eye to see clock and the data pin to the eye to see data. The Vcc must be five volts and ground to ground.

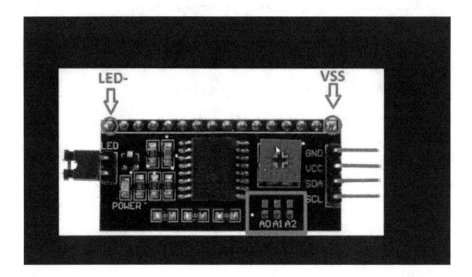

This is how the actual PCF 8574 looks like and as you can see, this end must be connected to the LCD VSS and the other end to the LED minus pin. By the way, you can control the LCD contrast using this potentiometer here.

This picture actually represents how the PC F is connected internally. This is very important to understand as our library will be written based on this connection diagram. As you can see, only the four pins p four to P seven are connected to the LCD data pins. The pins P zero, P one and P two are connected to the RS RW and enable pins respectively. Although it's not shown here, this pin p3 is actually connected to the LCD backlight. Now that we have seen the connection, let's check out the LCD 16 02 data sheet also, there are a lot of data sheets available, but things mostly remain the same across them. First of all, we will check the initialization part. As shown here. This is the pattern to initialize the LCD in four bit mode. We have seen in the connection diagram that only four pins from the PCF are actually connected to the data pins, and therefore we need to use the four bit mode for the LCD. As mentioned, first, we need to wait for more than 15 milliseconds and then we need to send this notice here that the eye spit represents whether we are sending a command all the data in order to send the command this bid must be zero, and to send the data it must be one.

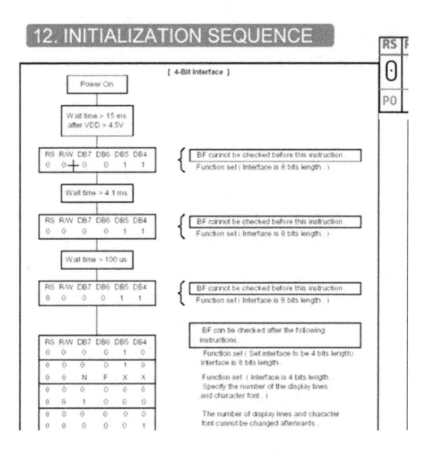

Also the RW bit indicates whether we are reading from the LCD or writing on it. In order to write something we must keep this bit zero. So here it means we are writing a commands to the LCD. Basically, the entire initialization sequence will be a set of commands. And that's why the RS and r w bits will always be zero. And now we are only provided with the bits D four to D seven, so we will keep the lower four bits as zeros. This will make the command zero cross three zero, then we need to wait for at least 4.1 milliseconds and send the same command again then wait for 100 microseconds and send the same command again.

Here you can see in the library I have performed the mentioned operations in a similar way now we will send another command that is zero cross to zero and it will set the interface to four bit length we are using the function LCD send command to send these commands to the display. Let's take a look at this function first. As the name suggests, the function can be used to send the commands to the LCD.

```c
/** Put this in the src folder **/

#include "i2c-lcd.h"
#include "esp_log.h"
#include "driver/i2c.h"
#include "unistd.h"

#define SLAVE_ADDRESS_LCD 0x4E>>1 // change this according to ur setup

esp_err_t err;

#define I2C_NUM I2C_NUM_0

static const char *TAG = "LCD";

void lcd_send_cmd (char cmd)
{
    char data_u, data_l;
    uint8_t data_t[4];
    data_u = (cmd&0xf0);
    data_l = ((cmd<<4)&0xf0);
    data_t[0] = data_u|0x0C;  //en=1, rs=0
    data_t[1] = data_u|0x08;  //en=0, rs=0
    data_t[2] = data_l|0x0C;  //en=1, rs=0
    data_t[3] = data_l|0x08;  //en=0, rs=0
    err = i2c_master_write_to_device(I2C_NUM, SLAVE_ADDRESS_LCD, data_t, 4, 1000);
    if (err!=0) ESP_LOGI(TAG, "Error in sending command");
}

void lcd_send_data (char data)
{
    char data_u, data_l;
    uint8_t data_t[4];
    data_u = (data&0xf0);
    data_l = ((data<<4)&0xf0);
    data_t[0] = data_u|0x0D;  //en=1, rs=0
    data_t[1] = data_u|0x09;  //en=0, rs=0
    data_t[2] = data_l|0x0D;  //en=1, rs=0
    data_t[3] = data_l|0x09;  //en=0, rs=0
```

It takes the eight bit command as the argument but since we are using the LCD in four bit mode, we have to send this eight bit command into two parts of four bit each. So

7

our first step would be to separate the upper half and lower half of this eight bit command. We will perform the end operation with the zero cross F zero and store this most significant half in the data you variable c manually, we will shift the command by four bits to the left position and then perform the operation with the zero cross F zero and store this least significant half in the data I variable. Now we need to add some other information to this command, which will include the RS bit, the R w bid and the backlight pin data, we will start preparing the final commands, and we will start by sending the most significant half first. Also remember that in order to send a command or data to the display, we need to provide something called the strobe. So after we send the data or the command, we pull the Enable pin high then pull it low. This strobe is a kind of signal to the LCD that we have set the respective data and now it can process it. Here in this library, I am sending the strobe along with the command itself. So basically, I am going to send the same command twice, once with the Enable pin high and the again with the Enable pin low. This means our P zero will be low to indicate that this is a command the P one will be low to indicate that we are performing a write operation and P two will be high to indicate that the Enable bit is high, and p three will be high so that the backlight remains on. This will make the command a zero cross zero C, and we will add it with our original command and store it in the first position, we will send the same command again, but this time the Enable pin will be low. So the first two bytes we write to the LCD will have the command along with the strobe. Similarly, we will store the least significant half in the other two bytes of the array. Finally, we are ready to send this array of four bytes to the LCD. Now we can use the respective eye to see function according to what controller you are using and send these four bytes to the LCD. So basically, we need the four bytes to send a single byte command. Similarly, to send the data to the display, we use this function LCD send data. It also takes the data byte as the argument and then we edit that data before sending four bytes. The only change we need to make his use the eyes bit as one to indicate that we are sending data this time. Other than that everything is similar to what we did while sending the command. So now that we know how to send data and commands to the display, let's continue with our initialization function. We have reached up to this part where we set the display into the four bit mode. The next few commands will be based on what kind of setup you want with the display. Notice here that now we have all the eight bytes for each command, and they all will be used in one way or another. Here we have the function set command. And to understand it, we need to see the instruction set in detail. Here the function set command and it sets the display mode, the number of rows and the font size. D L controls the display mode, one means eight bit mode, and zero means four bit mode, and controls the number of rows one means two rows, and

9

zero means only one row and the F controls the font size you want to use. I have already commented out everything I used in the library, and you are free to modify these parameters according to your convenience. The next command is the display switch command. Though it's not mentioned here, you can check it by the position of the one in the command. This command controls the display and the cursor, we have to first turn off the display as mentioned in the initialization sequence. The next command is to clear the display.

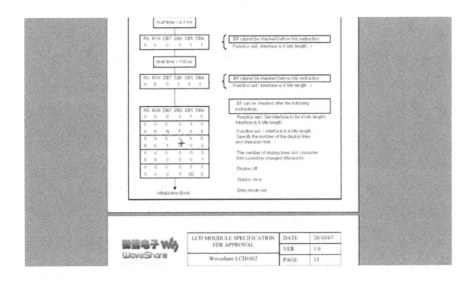

Here it is mentioned in the first position. Note that all these commands take some time to execute and therefore we must provide a small delay after each command the next command is to set the entry mode. Here we can control the movement of the cursor along with the shift in the display. I have set the cursor to increment and the display has no shift. If you turn on the display shift, you can control the shift direction by using this command later in the code. Finally, we will turn on the display by using the same command again. You can control the cursor and It's blinking. Also, the PDF I am using doesn't seem to be much detailed. So I would advise that you check a few other data sheets also, this entire sequence will initialize our LCD. Now we can use the LCD data send function to send one byte of data to the display. Remember that you can only send data in the ASCII format, so you can send a single character using this function. For example, LCD send data a or P or three, we have another function here, which can send the entire string to the display, it will simply call the send data function as long as all the characters from the string are printed. Now let's talk about the LCD put cursor function. This function sets the cursor at a specific location on the display. So the LCD have D D RAM addresses and only certain addresses are available to print these characters. I have covered this in the tutorial I wrote for the ESP 32. Here are the D D RAM addresses available for the LCD 16 02. The top row address starts from zero cross eight zero, and we can display 16 characters in this, the bottom row starts from zero cross c zero, and we can display another 16 characters in it. So this function takes the row and column as the parameter. And let's say if we want to print at the zero throw and fifth column. Since the zero throw starts from zero cross eight zero, it will add the column to this value, we will get the address zero cross eight five and we will send this as a command to the LCD indicating that we want to print at this address. Now if you send some data, it will display at this particular location. Similarly, if you give the input as first row and ninth column, it will add the column that is nine to zero cross c zero. This will result in the address zero cross C nine and then we can print at this particular location by sending the data next time. These are all the functions available in the library and I hope you understood how I wrote them. Now let's also talk about the slave address of the PCF 8574 device we are using. You can see the addresses defined here and I will explain why I am using this address. Let's check out the datasheet of the PCF 8574.

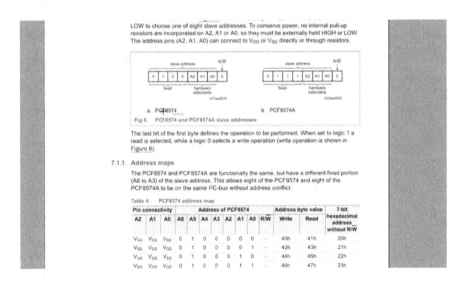

Here are the addresses defined for PCF a 574 or PCF 8574 A, I have the PCF 8574. So I will explain its address the four most significant bits of 0100 and then the next three bits are a zero, a one and a two. These three bits are responsible for controlling the address of the device. Here are the pins a zero, a one and a two and the pins next to them are ground. Right now the pins are high, and if we sold them to ground the respective pins goes low. The next bit we need to consider is the least significant bit which is the RW bit it is used along with the address to indicate whether we are performing the read or write to the device. So by default the addresses zero cross four E if we consider the readwrite bit and zero cross to seven if the readwrite bit is not taken into account. Depending on whether your MCU supports seven bit address or eight bit address, you can define it accordingly. So this is it for the project. I hope you understood how the library was written.

# EXAMPLE DUMMY CODE

Creating a complete I2C-LCD library involves writing code for both the LCD control and the I2C communication. Since writing an entire library is quite extensive, I can provide you with a basic outline and code snippets to get you started. Please note that this is a simplified example and might need adjustments based on the specific LCD module you are using and the microcontroller platform.

Library Outline:

Initialization:

Initialize the I2C communication.
Initialize the LCD module with appropriate settings.
Sending Commands and Data:

Write functions to send commands and data to the LCD module.
Display Control:

Functions to control display on/off, cursor visibility, cursor blinking, etc.
Text Handling:

Functions to write strings and characters to the LCD.
Positioning:

Functions to set the cursor position on the screen.
Custom Characters:

Functions to create and display custom characters.
Clearing and Home:

Functions to clear the display and return the cursor to the home position.
Examples:

Provide examples demonstrating how to use the library.
Here's a simplified example of what the library might look like:

```c
C
#include <Wire.h>

#define LCD_I2C_ADDR 0x27 // I2C address of the LCD module

// LCD commands
#define LCD_CMD_CLEAR        0x01
#define LCD_CMD_HOME         0x02
#define LCD_CMD_ENTRY_MODE   0x04
#define LCD_CMD_DISPLAY_CTRL  0x08
// ... other commands

class I2C_LCD {
public:
  I2C_LCD();
  void begin();
  void clear();
```

```cpp
  void home();
  void setCursor(uint8_t col, uint8_t row);
  void print(const char* text);
  void createCustomChar(uint8_t char_num,
uint8_t char_data[]);
  // ... other functions

private:
  void sendCommand(uint8_t command);
  void sendData(uint8_t data);
};

I2C_LCD::I2C_LCD() {
}

void I2C_LCD::begin() {
  Wire.begin();
  // Initialize LCD module (send necessary
commands)
}

void I2C_LCD::sendCommand(uint8_t command) {
  // Send command to LCD via I2C
}

void I2C_LCD::sendData(uint8_t data) {
  // Send data to LCD via I2C
}
```

```cpp
void I2C_LCD::clear() {
  sendCommand(LCD_CMD_CLEAR);
  // Add delay for LCD processing time
}

void I2C_LCD::home() {
  sendCommand(LCD_CMD_HOME);
  // Add delay for LCD processing time
}

void I2C_LCD::setCursor(uint8_t col, uint8_t row) {
  // Calculate and send cursor positioning
command
}

void I2C_LCD::print(const char* text) {
  // Iterate through text and send data bytes
}

void I2C_LCD::createCustomChar(uint8_t
char_num, uint8_t char_data[]) {
  // Send custom character creation commands
}

// Implementation of other functions...

// Example usage
```

```
I2C_LCD lcd;

void setup() {
  lcd.begin();
  lcd.print("Hello, I2C LCD!");
}

void loop() {
  // Your loop code here
}
```
Please note that this is a basic example to get you started. Depending on your LCD module's features and your requirements, you might need to implement additional functions and handle more complex commands. Also, ensure you adapt the library for your specific microcontroller platform and I2C address.

Remember that LCD modules and microcontrollers can vary in their implementation details, so you might need to refer to the datasheets and specifications for your specific components.

# COMMUNICATE WITH STONE HMI DISPLAY VIA THE UART

So we will be continuing with this series for a couple of more projects, I decided to go with the STM 32 First, and later I'll make more projects for Arduino and ESP 32. Also, since I need to do some basic explanation first, like what exactly do we get in the output when we press a button, or what data do we need to send in order for it to be displayed on the LCD. So I have decided to make an introductory project which will cover some basics about the data formatting of this HMI display. This project is not related to any microcontroller, but it's purely based on how we can control the display using the UART. Once you get the sense of it, we will start covering the microcontrollers one by one. Let's start with the project. Now. If you remember, in the end of the previous project, we discussed using the instruction sets to interface a microcontroller with this display. Well, we will take a look at that part again. But in a more detail and more practical way. Here is the picture of the PCB board that comes along with this display.

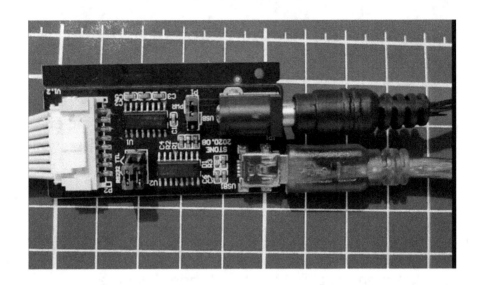

And you can see the connection. It is the same as we had in the previous project to the LCD basically communicates in the RS 232 format. But then we have the max 232 chip on this board, which will do the conversion to the TTL format. I have connected the mini USB between this board and the computer and you can see the con 13 in the Device Manager. Let's start the project and we will make a new project with the stone designer. By the way, the software is not available on their website, so you have to email them and hopefully they will send it to you go to the project. Select the new project. Give the name to the project, select Project folder, select screen size, keep the baud rate to 11 Five 200 and click Create. On the desktop here, I have two buttons and a background image which is resized to fit the display. To add the images to the project, under the Resources click on the image tab. Then click Add and select the images you want to add. I have all the

images in the PNG format here are all the images are
included in the project now to add the background image
we can drag and drop the image on the display. Let me set
the coordinates so that it fits the display properly. Not
much of the configuration is needed here just in the
background image section select the image all right now
we can see the image next we will add the buttons to the
display if you note here, the button size is 164 by 164.

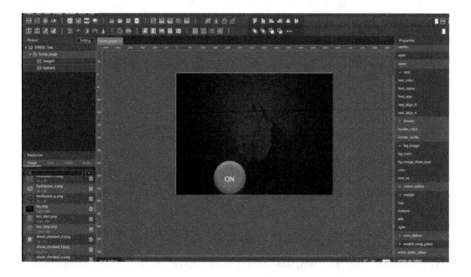

We will also use the same size for the button the button
has different states but first we will configure the normal
state the name of this button is button one the text on the
button will be on and let's use the default fonts the font
color will be white and the font size is 32. Choose the
background image for the button and we will make the
background transparent All right, let's adjust the margin a
little bit button still has a border around it. So I am making

it transparent. This was the setting for the normal mode. And when we press this button, it's going to look like this. Of course, we don't want this. And we will keep it similar to how it looked in the normal mode. So that means we need to configure everything again, so the button doesn't change when it's been pressed, except for the fact that I am giving a little bit of extra margin from the bottom. This makes the text shift a little upwards, and it will give us the feel of pressing the button. So we have configured the on button. And now we need to do the same for the off button. But since I don't want to go through the entire process again, we can just copy this and paste and here we have a copy of the on button. Now we will modify this a little and make it look like an off button. So the on button is the copy and the off button is the original one. All right now let's give some decent names to these buttons as these names are going to be a very important part of our code. For simplicity, I want to keep the names in a way that the length remains same for both. This will make it easier for us in the programming part. Of course, we can use names with different lengths, but you will see the advantage of this when we will write the code for the microcontroller. So the LEDs 01 is for the on button, and the LED 02 is for the off button. On pressing these button, the display will send the data via the UART. Now let's add one more element, which can display the data that it will receive from the UART label is the element which is used to print some string or a value on this display. A little bit of configuration is needed here. All right, everything is done. Now save the project, and then click debug download. And now we will choose the project folder the project has been saved. Now we need to copy the project into the display. So go to the project folder. There you will see this default folder, copy this and paste it in the mass storage folder of the stone display. This is it. Now we just need to reset the display. But before that, let's open the serial monitor. The USB is connected to come 13. Let's also open the instruction set. This is instruction set 1.5. And you can get it from the support page under the user manual. This will help us with the understanding of how the data is transmitted between the MCU and the display. Here is how the MCU needs to send the data to the display. The data must consist of the frame header, then the data itself and the frame tail in the end. Similarly, when the display sends the data to the MCU, it sends the header then the command then the length of the data then the data itself followed by the frame tail and two bytes of CRC. We will see this in working in a while. All right, let's reset the module now. The new project is loaded successfully. All right, let's click the on button. You can see some weird characters on the serial monitor. Let's change this data to hex. Now we have a better understanding of what has been received and we will understand it more through the instruction set manual. Let's check the button section. Here you can see the format for the button response.

If we change the data back to the ASCII format, we can see something similar on the monitor. The first three bytes are the frame header, and then we have the data starting with 1001. Everything has been explained in detail like this particular instruction represents the system key delivery. Here we have the same. The next two bytes represent the length of the data, which is the combination of the widget name and its value. In our case we have the length of six bytes. This is the length of the widget name and its value As per the data we received, the widgets name is LED 01, which is five bytes, and one byte is for the value, the value of the widget is one. Then we have the next three bytes for the frame tail, which will be the same for everything. And finally the last two bytes for the CRC. This completes one data frame when the button is pressed. But soon after pressing the button, we released it. And that's why we have another data frame, which consists of exactly the same format except the value here is two. So when we press the button, the value is one and when we release it, the value is two. This completes the button click event. So if I keep the button in pressed state, one complete frame will be transmitted and you can see the value is one. And when I release this button, another frame is transmitted with the value two. If we press the off button, exactly the same thing will happen. But this time the button name is LEDs 02. Basically, when we will interface this with our micro controller, we will look for these button names, and based on what Button Was Clicked, we will change the state of the LED. Now let's do the label. The label can be used to print the text on the display or print some value. We will try both but let's start with the text. This here is the data frame we need to send in order to print the text on the label. Before we send this data frame, let's understand this. We start with the frame header followed by the command code, which is set text since we want to print the text. Then we have the type of the element which is the label in our case, then the name of the widget followed by what text you want to print. And finally the frame tail to indicate the end of the data. We have the widget name as label one the one we input while creating the label.

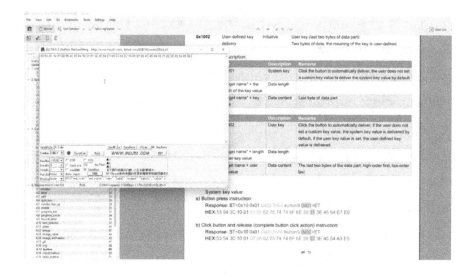

This here will be the text that will be printed on the label. Press Send to send the data to the display. You can see the text printed on the display. The buttons work as usual without any issues. Let's print hello world instead of just like text, we can directly print the numerical values. Let's change this to label one and send this here we have the value printed on the display so we saw what data the display sends when we press the buttons on it and what data do we need to send in order to display some text or value on it? We will utilize this information when we will interface this with our microcontroller. We will continue with the STM 32 first and then later move to ESP 32. And finally Arduino.

# STEPPER MOTOR USING THE POTENTIOMETER WAVE DRIVE ROTARY ANGLE SENSOR

I have downloaded this stepper motor code from my old project I will use this with some minor changes and I will explain them as we go along. So let's start by creating a project in cube Id first I will be using my usual F 446 r e give some name to this project and click finish first of all I am setting the external crystal for the clock. Let's set the clock now. I have eight megahertz Crystal and I am running the system at 90 megahertz. Note here that both of the APB clocks are at 90 megahertz.

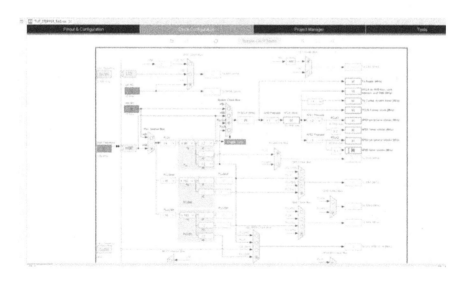

The reason I am saying this is because we will be using the microsecond delay and if both APB timer clocks are running at 90, this means all the timers will also be running at 90 megahertz and it will be easier to remember this here is the nucleo pin out I am going to use this pa one as the ADC input for the potentiometer these four pins p are for PB zero, PC One and PC zero will be used as the output pins to the stepper motor. Let's set them now enable the respective ADC channel. We will be using D ama today so let's enable it choose the circular mode. Now let's go back to ADC setup. Here we have 12 bit ADC scan conversion is not needed. Since we are only using single channel enable the continuous conversion and the DM or continuous request. This completes the ADC setup. Now let's set those four pins as output. Now we will configure a timer for microsecond delay. I am choosing timer six. Both our APB timer clocks are at 90 megahertz. So use the prescaler of 90 to bring down this clock to one megahertz use the highest possible value in the auto reload register so that our timer could never hit this this completes our setup click Save to generate the code let's see the code from that previous stepper motor project we will use pretty much all these functions we have used half drive last time but we will use something else this time.

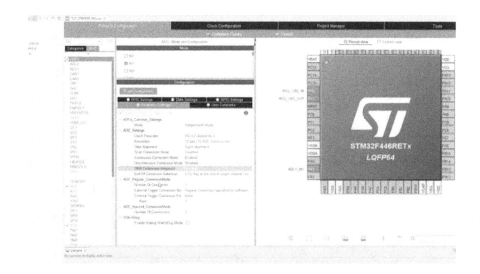

Let's start define the pins according to how they are connected to the stepper motor. As you can see here, the steps per revolution are defined as 4096 here.

This is because we use the half drive in that project. In my article I did covered that stepper motor can use three drives. In half drive, two electromagnets are energized at a time. But if you see the wave drive here, only one magnet is energized at a time so it's less complex to use. The steps in one revolution are 2048 Compared to 4096 in half drive but remember guys wave drive also have less torque compared to half drive let's define the number of steps per revolution copy the function to set the stepper motor RPM we will use this as it is we need to copy the delay function also here I am using the timer six instead of timer one I have defined two functions to set and reset the respective pins instead of the half drive we will be using the wave drive here if you need more torque, you can still use the half drive from that stepper motor project.

```
File  Edit  Source  Refactor  Navigate  Search  Project  Run  Window  Help

        HAL_GPIO_WritePin(GPIOx, GPIO_PIN, GPIO_PIN_SET));
    }

    void ResetPin (GPIO_TypeDef* GPIOx, uint16_t GPIO_Pin)
    {
        HAL_GPIO_WritePin(GPIOx, GPIO_Pin, GPIO_PIN_RESET);
    }

    void stepper_wave_drive (int step)
    {
        switch (step){
            case 0:
                SetPin(IN1Port, IN1Pin);    // IN1 SET
                ResetPin(IN2Port, IN2Pin);  // IN2 RESET
                ResetPin(IN3Port, IN3Pin);  // IN3 RESET
                ResetPin(IN4Port, IN4Pin);  // IN4 RESET
                break;

            case 1:
                ResetPin(IN1Port, IN1Pin);  // IN1 RESET
                SetPin(IN2Port, IN2Pin);    // IN2 SET
                ResetPin(IN3Port, IN3Pin);  // IN3 RESET
                ResetPin(IN4Port, IN4Pin);  // IN4 RESET
                break;

            case 2:
                ResetPin(IN1Port, IN1Pin);  // IN1 RESET
                ResetPin(IN2Port, IN2Pin);  // IN2 RESET
                SetPin(IN3Port, IN3Pin);    // IN3 SET
                ResetPin(IN4Port, IN4Pin);  // IN4 RESET
                break;

            case 3:
                ResetPin(IN1Port, IN1Pin);  // IN1 RESET
                ResetPin(IN2Port, IN2Pin);  // IN2 RESET
                ResetPin(IN3Port, IN3Pin);  // IN3 RESET
                SetPin(IN4Port, IN4Pin);    // IN4 SET

            }
    }
```

As you can see in Wave drive, only one pin is set at a time and this will energize only one magnet at a time. Next, we will copy the step angle function as it is here we calculate the angle by which the motor will rotate in one sequence. Basically there are 512 sequences in one complete rotation and this remains same for whatever drive you use. Then based on the angle we calculate the number of sequences and finally the motor will rotate based on the provided direction now let's define some new variables that we are going to use in this project. ADC vowel will store the ADC value, which will be then converted to the voltage which will be further converted to the angle current angle will keep track of the angle which the motor is currently at. This is to make sure that motor rotates only by the change in angle and not the actual angle. Now the stepper rotate will do the calculation for the angle and the direction in which the motor needs to rotate. Here we will first calculate the change in angle. If this change is positive, then the motor will rotate in the clockwise direction by the amount that has been changed similarly, if the change is negative, it will first calculate the positive version of this change and then the motor will rotate counterclockwise by the changed amount. Then the angle value will be stored in the current angle now we will write the ADC conversion callback which will be called whenever the DMA conversion is complete. Here is the function for the callback first we will calculate the voltage from the potentiometer then convert this voltage to the angle I am using 300 Because that's the maximum amount by which my angle sensor can rotate. And now we will call the stepper rotate to rotate the motor by the angle that we got from the sensor. I am using this RPM of 10 it should be kept below 14 Let's write the main function now. First of all we will stop Time Timer then start the ADC in the DMA mode let's build it now. Seems like we got some errors here Oh, I forgot to change this to wave drive let's build again it's okay now, except this warning. This is the answer to the question you guys have always asked me in the ADC project. That why did I use 32 bit variable when the ADC is 12 bit This is the reason for that this function takes 32 bit variable as the parameter and that's why I use the 32 bit variable but today I am using 16 bit and it's throwing this warning anyway, we can neglect this warning let's debug our code I am going to add all the variables in the live expression okay, let's run it now. As you can see the motor is rotating by the proper angle in the respective direction.

But I see some shift in the zero position here. I think the motor is not able to freely rotate in one direction. And this could be due to the fact that I am using voltage source from the microcontroller. If you guys also see this error, let me know in the comments. I will update the code according to that. One last thing before I wrap up this project. If the motor is too shaky, increase this change in angle to two or maybe three. This happens because the ADC readings are unstable and it's not that easy to stabilize them using some code. You can try some hardware hacks though, try googling it. This is it for this project. I hope things were clear.

# EXAMPLE DUMMY CODE

Controlling a stepper motor using a potentiometer (for speed control) and a rotary angle sensor (for position control) involves using a microcontroller and a stepper motor driver. Here's an example code using an Arduino and the AccelStepper library to achieve this. In this example, the potentiometer is used to control the speed of the stepper motor, and the rotary angle sensor is used to control the position.

Install AccelStepper Library:
Open the Arduino IDE, go to "Sketch" -> "Include Library" -> "Manage Libraries", and search for "AccelStepper". Install the library.

Wiring:
Connect your stepper motor and sensors according to their specifications. Here's a simplified wiring guide:

Stepper Motor Driver (e.g., A4988):

Connect motor coils to the driver's output pins.
Connect stepper motor driver's control pins (STEP and DIR) to Arduino pins.
Connect stepper motor driver's ENABLE pin to an Arduino pin (optional).
Potentiometer:

Connect one end to 5V.
Connect the other end to GND.
Connect the middle pin (wiper) to an analog input pin on the Arduino.
Rotary Angle Sensor (e.g., Rotary Encoder):

Connect CLK pin to an interrupt-capable Arduino pin.
Connect DT pin to another interrupt-capable Arduino pin.
Connect SW pin (if available) to an Arduino pin.
Example Code:
Here's a basic example code that demonstrates

controlling a stepper motor using a potentiometer for speed and a rotary angle sensor (encoder) for position control. Make sure to adjust pin numbers and other settings according to your wiring and components.

**Arduino**

```
#include <AccelStepper.h>

// Define stepper motor connections
#define STEP_PIN 2
#define DIR_PIN 3
#define ENABLE_PIN 4 // Set to -1 if not used

// Define analog input pin for potentiometer
#define POT_PIN A0

// Define rotary encoder pins
#define ENC_CLK_PIN 5
#define ENC_DT_PIN 6
#define ENC_SW_PIN 7

// Create stepper motor instance
AccelStepper stepper(AccelStepper::DRIVER,
STEP_PIN, DIR_PIN);

void setup() {
// Set up pins
 pinMode(POT_PIN, INPUT);
```

```
pinMode(ENC_SW_PIN, INPUT_PULLUP); // If
using a switch on the encoder

attachInterrupt(digitalPinToInterrupt(ENC_CLK_PIN
), updatePosition, CHANGE);

attachInterrupt(digitalPinToInterrupt(ENC_DT_PIN)
, updatePosition, CHANGE);

// Set up stepper motor
stepper.setMaxSpeed(2000); // Adjust this value
stepper.setAcceleration(1000); // Adjust this value

// Set initial position (if needed)
stepper.setCurrentPosition(0);
}

void loop() {
// Read potentiometer value and map it to a
speed range
int potValue = analogRead(POT_PIN);
int speed = map(potValue, 0, 1023, 0, 2000); //
Adjust speed range

// Update stepper motor speed
stepper.setSpeed(speed);

// Handle encoder switch (if used for position
```

```
control)
 if (digitalRead(ENC_SW_PIN) == LOW) {
  stepper.setCurrentPosition(0); // Reset position
on switch press
 }

 // Move the stepper motor continuously (remove
if not needed)
 stepper.runSpeed();
}

void updatePosition() {
 // Handle encoder position update here
 // For example, you can increase/decrease
position based on encoder rotation direction
 int encoderState = (digitalRead(ENC_CLK_PIN) <<
1) | digitalRead(ENC_DT_PIN);
 // Update stepper position based on encoderState
}
```

This code provides a basic framework for
controlling a stepper motor using a potentiometer
for speed control and a rotary angle sensor
(encoder) for position control. You'll need to adapt
the code to your specific components and
requirements, and you might want to add more
features like limiting the position range or adding
additional buttons for control.

# DELAY IN NANO MICRO SECONDS USING TIMERS IN STM32

Although it worked perfectly, there were some microcontrollers, which does not support DWT specially the F zero series and the f3 series microcontrollers. So today in this project I will show you how to generate delay in microseconds and nanoseconds across all the STM 32 controllers and to do so I am going to use the timers let's start with the cube MX first I am using STM 32 Cube IDE. Okay now the clock is set to the maximum. Note that the APB to clock is at 180 megahertz and the APB one clock is at 90 megahertz.

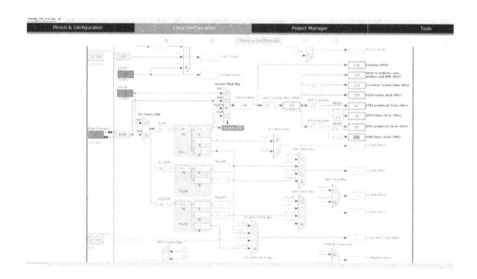

Now, let's take a look at the timers in the datasheet. Note that timer one is connected to the APB two. So I am going to use that for the delay. Because in order to create delay in nanosecond, I need at least 100 megahertz clock frequency for the timer set the timer at 100 megahertz.

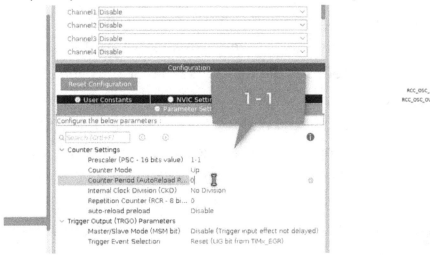

Now like I said, I need 100 megahertz for the delay in nanoseconds and it will give me a delay of 10 nanoseconds. Unfortunately, I cannot go lower than that. So the prescaler value is going to be zero because we can not divide the APB clock any further. I am writing one one minus one just to indicate that whatever value is input here, the micro controller is going to add one to it. So our actual value is one and we are subtracting one for the micro controller to added later. The auto reload register for time one is 16 bit so I will input the maximum value here and that is zero cross F FFF, which turns out to be 65,536 in decimals.

```
47  /* USER CODE BEGIN PV */
48
49  /* USER CODE END PV */
50
51  /* Private function prototypes ---------------------------
52  void SystemClock_Config(void);
53  static void MX_GPIO_Init(void);
54  static void MX_TIM1_Init(void);
55  /* USER CODE BEGIN PFP */
56
57  /* USER CODE END PFP */
58
59  /* Private user code ------------------------------
60  /* USER CODE BEGIN 0 */
61
62  void delay (uint16_t delay)
63  {
64      __HAL_TIM_SET_COUNTER (&htim1, 0);
65      while ( __HAL_TIM_GET_COUNTER(&htim1) b
66  }
67
68  /* USER CODE END 0 */
69
70  /**
71    * @brief  The application entry point.
72    * @retval int
73    */
74  int main(void)
75  {
76      /* USER CODE BEGIN 1 */
77
78      /* USER CODE END 1 */
79
80
81      /* MCU Configuration---------------------------
```

Also, I am setting pin p one as output so that we can measure the frequency in an oscilloscope. Let's write the code now. Okay, first of all, I will create a function for the delay whose parameter is going to be the delay we want. Remember that if you input value one here, that's going to be a 10 nanoseconds delay, because our clock is at 100 megahertz. Inside this function, we will set the counter to zero and then let the counter increment until it reaches the input value that we have provided. Each count takes 10 nanoseconds in this case, once it does, the control will come out from the loop. Also remember that we cannot use the delay higher than 65,536 because that's the limit for our counter as it is only 16 bits. If you want higher values, you have to use a 32 bit timer. But in my case, the maximum clock to the 32 bit timers is 90 megahertz, so I couldn't use it. Now inside the main function, let's toggle the pin after some delay So if the delay is one that's going to be 10 nanoseconds now 100 nanoseconds, 1000 nanoseconds, which is one microsecond, 10 microseconds, 100 microseconds, I am using this higher delay, because I don't have means to measure the high frequencies. So this 100 microseconds is going to give me a frequency of 10 kilohertz, which I can measure. But as the pin will toggle after every 100 microseconds, the oscilloscope is going to read it as five kilohertz because this one reads the frequency of pin toggling.

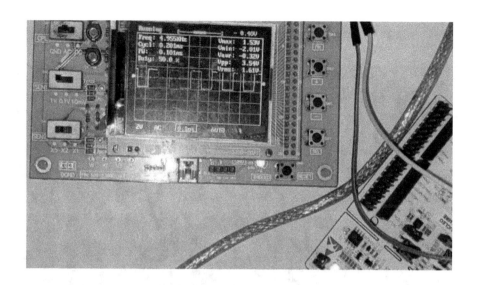

Make sure you initialize the timer in its normal mode. Let's build this code and test it. If you want one nanoseconds delay, your controller frequency should be at least one gigahertz. Similarly, if you want the delay in microseconds, all you have to do is use the prescaler to divide the main time clock to get a one megahertz frequency. So, the prescaler value in that case would be 100 minus one. As you can see here, the frequency is five kilohertz that means the nanosecond delay is working as it should. Let me reduce the delay a little so that we can increase the frequency. Now I am using 50 microseconds delay. Technically, this should give me the frequency of 20 kilohertz but like I said, the oscilloscope is going to read the frequency of pin toggling. It is going to read it as 10 kilohertz.

# EXAMPLE DUMMY CODE

here's an example of how you can create delays in nanoseconds and microseconds using timers on an STM32 microcontroller. In this example, I'll be using the STM32 HAL (Hardware Abstraction Layer) library to demonstrate the code. Please note that the exact code might vary depending on the specific STM32 series and HAL version you are using.

C

```c
#include "stm32f4xx_hal.h"

// Timer and clock configuration
TIM_HandleTypeDef htim2; // Change this to the appropriate timer instance
uint32_t SystemCoreClock = 16000000; // Change this to your system's core clock frequency

// Initialize the timer
void TIM2_Init(void) {
 htim2.Instance = TIM2; // Change to the appropriate timer instance
 htim2.Init.Prescaler = (SystemCoreClock / 1000000) - 1; // Timer increments every microsecond
```

```c
  htim2.Init.CounterMode =
TIM_COUNTERMODE_UP;
  htim2.Init.Period = 0xFFFFFFFF; // Maximum
period to get the longest delay possible
  htim2.Init.ClockDivision =
TIM_CLOCKDIVISION_DIV1;
  HAL_TIM_Base_Init(&htim2);
}

// Delay in nanoseconds
void DelayNano(uint32_t ns) {
  __HAL_TIM_SET_COUNTER(&htim2, 0);
  while (__HAL_TIM_GET_COUNTER(&htim2) < ns)
{
   // Wait
  }
}

// Delay in microseconds
void DelayMicro(uint32_t us) {
  DelayNano(us * 1000);
}

int main(void) {
  HAL_Init();
  SystemClock_Config();
  TIM2_Init();
```

```
// Your code here

while (1) {
 // Delay for 1 microsecond
 DelayMicro(1);

 // Your main loop code here
 }
}
```

In this code, we use Timer 2 as an example timer instance. You would need to adapt the code according to your STM32 microcontroller's specific timer options. The DelayNano function uses the timer to create a delay in nanoseconds, and the DelayMicro function utilizes the DelayNano function to create a delay in microseconds.

Please consult your STM32 reference manual, datasheet, and HAL documentation for accurate information on timer configurations and clock settings for your specific microcontroller model.

# DISPLAY ANIMATION ON NEXTION

Here is a GIF that I will be using in this project. You can also use this same logic for displaying gauges or projects.

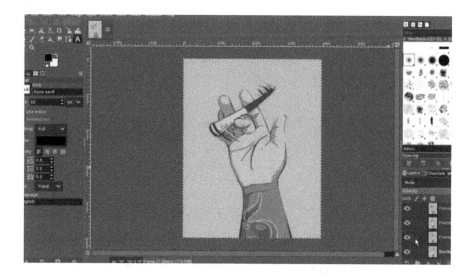

Let's open this GIF with GIMP you can see here that we have 21 frames for this particular GIF first of all I will reduce the image size so that it fits the display I am going to display it in the vertical orientation so 240 will be the width and 320 is the height so now all the frames have been scaled to this size let's hide all the frames except the very first one now export this image I am exporting it to the JPEG format you can use any other to check the manual for the supported formats now hide the first frame unhide the second frame and export it to you have to do the same for all the frames I have already done it and here are all the 21 frames let's go back to the next in editor create a new project choose your display here. Like I said I am using vertical orientation here is our display.

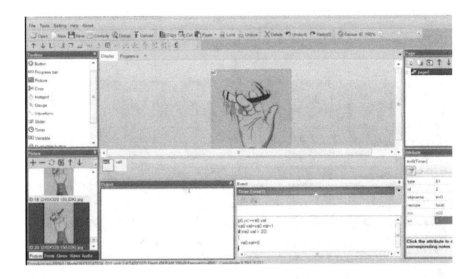

First of all I will add the picture element to it also we need to add all those pictures here select all of them and hit enter you can see the first one have the ID zero and the last one have the ID 20. Let's add the first picture to this element now in order to change the pictures, we will add a timer and a variable let's write some code for the timer here we will load the respective number of image to the P zero element. As you can see the default value of the variable is zero so the image with ID zero will be loaded first. Now increment the variables value. This will also increment the image ID when the first statement gets executed next time and a new image will be displayed as we We only have 21 images so we should also limit the variable value to 20 and if the value goes higher than 20 it will be back to zero again this here is the time delay between each image and let's keep it a little less let's build it now.

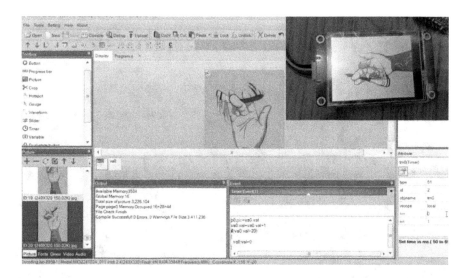

Looks like we got some error here. I shouldn't have put the space in between another error no termination also great. It compiles successfully now let's debug it this looks pretty good let's try to increase the time delay this does not look satisfying at all I am going to reduce it to the minimum value and that is 50 In my case now let's upload it to the board here is the connection between the display and the FTDI the blue wire is connected between the display Tx and the device RX and yellow wire his other way around red is with five volts and back to ground click Go to stop the upload it have started so the upload is done. And here we have our gift being played on the display I will increase the time delay a little more let's upload again it looks pretty sweet. Now. This particular display have the minimum time delay of 50 milliseconds so it can support up to 20 frames per second.

# EXAMPLE DUMMY CODE

To create a display animation on a Nextion display, you'll need to design the animation in the Nextion Editor software and then use the Nextion library in your microcontroller code to control and trigger the animation. Below is a simplified example using an Arduino and the Nextion library.

Please make sure you have the Nextion Editor installed to design your animation and export the necessary files.

Design Animation in Nextion Editor:

Create your animation in the Nextion Editor. Define the animation components (like pictures, buttons, text) that will be part of your animation sequence.
Set up the animation settings, like frame delays, transition effects, etc.
Export the Nextion project and obtain the .tft file.
Upload .tft File to Nextion Display:

Use the Nextion Editor's built-in upload tool to upload the .tft file to your Nextion display module.
Arduino Code Example:
Here's a simple Arduino code example that demonstrates how to trigger an animation on a Nextion display using the Nextion library.

```cpp
#include <Nextion.h>

NexDSButton bt_animation = NexDSButton(0, 2, "bt_animation"); // Replace with your component's details

void setup() {
 Serial.begin(9600);
 nexInit(); // Initialize Nextion communication
}

void loop() {
 nexLoop(nex_listen_list); // Listen for events

 // Trigger animation when button is pressed
 if (bt_animation.getValue() == 1) {
  // Send command to start animation on Nextion display
  nexSerial.print("t0.pco=63488"); // Change the
```

```
component ID accordingly
 nexSerial.write(0xFF);
 nexSerial.write(0xFF);
 nexSerial.write(0xFF);
 bt_animation.setValue(0); // Reset button state
 }
}
```

In this code, replace the bt_animation definition with the appropriate details of your component from the Nextion Editor. The code listens for button presses on the Nextion display. When the button is pressed, it sends a command to start the animation. The t0.pco command changes the background color of the component with the specified ID, which is a way to trigger animations on Nextion displays.

Remember to adjust the code according to your specific Nextion display and the animation you've designed. Additionally, you might need to incorporate additional logic to control the animation timing, transitions, and more advanced interactions.

Always refer to the Nextion documentation, library, and your specific display's specifications for accurate details and usage instructions.

# STM32F103 AS A MOUSE CUBEIDE USB HID DEVICE

I will show you guys how to emulate STM 32 F 103 aka blue pill as a mouse to control the cursor on your computer. This is more like a gravity mouse as it involves the accelerometer from which we get the accelerations in x and y directions. The mouse movement will be based on these acceleration values. Let's start by creating a new project in cube ID. Give some name to the project and click finish here is our cube MX first of all I am selecting external crystal for the clock. Next select serial wire debug.

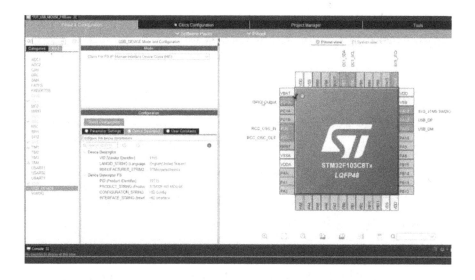

Now I am selecting the i two c one to connect the ad XL 345 accelerometer Next, select USB and enabled device F s I am leaving everything to default here in the USB device select the class as h ID class you can leave everything default I am changing the name to show that it actually works. This is the name for my device and this will pop up in the computer after I connect the USB let's enable the onboard LED also we will use it as an indication select the pin PA seven as the XD pin as I will connect the button to it let's go to the GP i o setup P A seven is the external interrupt pin where the mouse button will be connected to this is how I am going to connect the button when the button is pressed the 3.3 volts will feed to the pin PA seven and the MCU will detect a high in the input I know the current will sink into the pin PA seven but as we are only using the 3.3 volts from the MCU itself this current won't be that much I am changing the trigger to falling edge you can use the rising edge also. I am using pull down here because I want this pin to act as a ground for the input current also change the output of PC 13 to high so that the LED is often default state I am setting the max clock for the system let's check if everything is covered. We have USB by to see led button. I forgot to enable the interrupt for the SD line. Now all is okay so let's save this to generate the project by the time we will look into the connections ad XL 345 is connected via the eye to see with pins B six and B seven. It is powered with 3.3 volts from the MCU itself. Here we have our main file let's first include the usph ID dot h File Open the USB device dot c and copy the USB handle type def from here I have created a structure for mouse data which includes button x value, y value and the wheel it should be created in the same order I am initializing everything with the zero let's create the ad x I related functions. I have already covered these in the previous projects, you can check it on the top right corner.

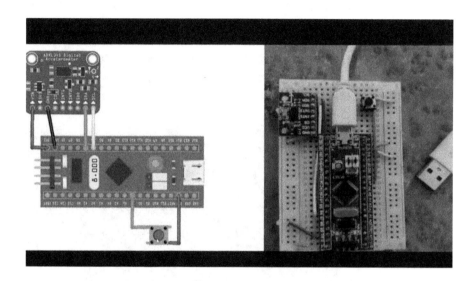

Before proceeding further, let's declare some variables that we are going to use. These are the minimum and maximum values for x and y. These will change after we calibrate the sensor button flag will be used in the interrupt handler. Here is the function to calibrate the ADX cell values. I am reading the ad Excel raw values after taking 50 samples this function will set the new Max and new minimum values this whole process will take five seconds and once completed the LED on board will light up to indicate the completion now let's write for the external interrupt. We need the XT callback function for this if the interrupt is triggered by the pin PA seven then set the button flag to one rest of the processing for the button will be done in the while loop let's move to the main function now. Initialize the ADX cell calibrated now in the while loop, we will get new X and Y values if the x value is less than the minimum x value, we have our new x value, which is the difference between them. And if the x value is greater than the maximum x value, then the new x value will be the difference between them.

This is basically to make sure that the little movement of the sensor doesn't get updated as the mouse movement. We do the similar things for the y values. Let's give a delay of 10 milliseconds first we will test this part of the code to make sure the data is correct. And as per our requirement. Let's build this code and debug it right now the sensor is calibrating for my orientation. Green light is on so the calibration is done. Check the values here we have new max values and new minimum values. Note that when I tilt towards right the y values are increasing in positive way. tilting towards left and wide values are negative tilting towards the front X becomes negative and towards back x becomes positive. In this diagram, the red color is computers axis and green color is our values, as you can see in the right direction computer have positive X axis and we have positive y values and in the upward direction computer have negative y values and we have negative x values. So all we need to do is send the sensors y values to the x coordinate of the mouse and sensors X values to the y coordinates of the mouse if the variation in the x values is more than 20, we will send the value to the y coordinate of the mouse and the same for the x coordinate of the mouse, here I chose 20 And you can choose any other number also, based on how sensitive you want the mouse to be. If the values are less than 20, there will be no changes in the coordinates now our data is ready to be sent to the USB send report function is used to send the data to the USB let's build this we have a warning, but that's okay. Let's debug our code now. I will directly run this let's open the device manager or better open the devices in the settings. I am opening the devices to show you how the mouse will be detected. Let's connect the USB now.

```
192     y = ((Rx_Data[3]<<8)|Rx_Data[2]);
193     z = ((Rx_Data[5]<<8)|Rx_Data[4]);
194
195     if (x < min_xval) newxval = x - min_xval;
196     if (x > max_xval) newxval = x - max_xval;
197     if (y < min_yval) newyval = y - min_yval;
198     if (y > max_yval) newyval = y - max_yval;
199
200     if ((newxval > 20) || (newxval < -20))
201     {
202         mousehid.mouse_y = newxval/3;
203     }
204                                int16_t newxval = 0;
                                   Press F2 for focus
205     else mousehid.mouse_y = 0;
206
207     if ((newyval > 20) || (newyval < -20))
208     {
209         mousehid.mouse_x = newyval/3;
210     }
211
212     else mousehid.mouse_x = 0;
213
214     if (button_flag == 1)
215     {
216         mousehid.button = 1;  // left click =1, right click =2
217         USBD_HID_SendReport(&hUsbDeviceFS, &mousehid, sizeof (mousehid));
218         HAL_Delay(50);
219         mousehid.button = 0;  // left click =1, right click =2
220         USBD_HID_SendReport(&hUsbDeviceFS, &mousehid, sizeof (mousehid));
221         button_flag = 0;
222     }
223
224
225     USBD_HID_SendReport(&hUsbDeviceFS, &mousehid, sizeof (mousehid));
226
227
228     HAL_Delay(10);
229 }
```

Problems  Tasks  Console  Properties
TUT_USB_MOUSE_F103 Debug [STM32 Cortex-M C/C++ Application] ST-LINK (ST-LINK GDB server)
    Status Refresh Delay        : 15s
    Verbose Mode                : Disabled
    SWD Debug                   : Enabled
    InitWhile                   : Enabled

As you can see STM 32 F 103 mouse gets detected here. It's been detected in the mouse or keyboard category. Also, Windows is detecting it as a mouse. As I lift it up, you can see the cursor is moving. But let's reset it once so the code can calibrate sensor for this orientation LED is on so the calibration is done. You can see the movement is as per the tilting of the device. But this acceleration is too fast. I want to slow this down. To do so I need to reduce these values. So I am dividing them by three. You can choose any other device or based on how much acceleration you want. We also need to add the button to the mouse. If you remember in the interrupt callback function, we set the button flag. Now, if the button flag is one, we will write value one to the button of the mouse value one indicates the left click. If you want to emulate the right click Write the value two. After writing the value, send the report to indicate the click. We also need to send the button value is zero to indicate the button was released. Let's add a delay of 50 milliseconds between these reports. So first click and then released and in the end, set the button flag to zero. Let's build and run now. Again we will do the calibration first you can see movement is pretty smooth the button works too. I have found out that this button works better if we set the rising edge trigger to the external interrupt so you can try that if you have some issues anyway single click and double click works all right he also this is it for this project. I hope you understood the process. You can use any other accelerometer also, for example, g y 521 or something similar.

# EXAMPLE DUMMY CODE

Creating a USB HID device using the STM32F103 microcontroller in CubeIDE involves configuring the USB HID class and defining the necessary endpoints for communication. Below is an example code that demonstrates how to set up the STM32F103 as a USB HID mouse using the STM32CubeIDE software.

Please note that this example provides a simplified overview and might need to be adapted to your specific requirements and hardware configuration.

Create a New Project:

Open STM32CubeIDE and create a new project for your STM32F103 microcontroller.
Configure the Clock settings and other necessary configurations.
Configure USB HID:

Open the "USB_DEVICE" configuration in STM32CubeMX.
Enable the "Human Interface Device (HID)" middleware and configure it for the mouse application.
Configure the endpoints and other settings as

needed.
Generate Code:

Generate the code using STM32CubeMX.
Implement the Mouse Logic:

Open the generated project in STM32CubeIDE.
Locate the usb_device.c file and implement the
mouse functionality.
Here's a simplified example code that
demonstrates a basic USB HID mouse using the
STM32F103 microcontroller:

C

```c
#include "usb_device.h"

USBD_HandleTypeDef hUsbDeviceFS;

void SystemClock_Config(void);
static void MX_GPIO_Init(void);

int16_t x_mouse = 0; // Mouse X coordinate
int16_t y_mouse = 0; // Mouse Y coordinate

int main(void) {
 HAL_Init();
 SystemClock_Config();
```

```
MX_GPIO_Init();

MX_USB_DEVICE_Init();

while (1) {
 // Update mouse coordinates and send the HID
report
 USBD_HID_SendReport(&hUsbDeviceFS,
(uint8_t*)&x_mouse, 3); // Send X and Y
movement
 HAL_Delay(10); // Delay to control mouse
movement speed
 }
}

void SystemClock_Config(void) {
 // Configure the system clock as needed
}

static void MX_GPIO_Init(void) {
 // Configure GPIO pins as needed
}

void HAL_SYSTICK_Callback(void) {
 // Update mouse coordinates here, e.g., based on
sensor input
 // Modify x_mouse and y_mouse values
}
```

```
void EXTI15_10_IRQHandler(void) {
// Handle interrupts for buttons or sensors that
trigger mouse clicks
// Modify the HID report to send mouse button
information
HAL_GPIO_EXTI_IRQHandler(GPIO_PIN_13); //
Adjust the pin number accordingly
}
```

Please note that this is a simplified example, and you'll need to modify and enhance it according to your requirements. You should refer to the STM32F1 reference manual, CubeIDE documentation, and USB HID specifications for accurate details on setting up USB HID devices.

Additionally, you need to ensure that your hardware is properly connected, including proper clock settings, GPIO configuration, and any additional hardware components required for your application.

# GENERATE WAVEFORMS ON NEXTION DISPLAY STM32 SINE WAVE SQUARE WAVE

I will be using my STM 32 for sending the sine wave and the square waves of different frequencies. Let's start by creating a new project in nexty and editor give some name to the project here. Select your display type and the display orientation that you want to work with. I am going to add a wave form here and resize it to fit the whole display here we have the ID one you can change the grid width and height here I will change it back to 40 that fits my display better you can select how many channels you want to work with. I will use two channels to show the difference between the two. That's basically all let's debug this once I will send the waveform to this display that's how it's going to look. Each grid here represents 40 And that's why the lowest point is 40 As I have used it as the minimum value let's upload it to the board here I am using a ftdi module two upload the code the blue wire is connected between the display TX to the module RX and the yellow is between the display RX to the module TX red is five volts and black is ground. Let's upload the code now.

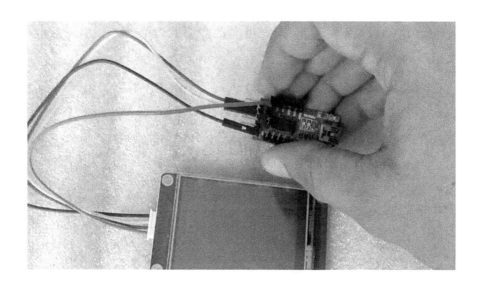

It's uploaded and the editor part is done now. Let's open the cube ID and create a new project I am using a 446 r e i am selecting external crystal for the main clock. IMU using you up for to send data to the display change the baud rate to 9600. In the clock setup, I have external eight megahertz Crystal and I want the system to run at maximum clock click Save to generate the project so here is our main file. I am adding these and commands that we need to send to the display after we are done with sending data. Now we need to send the values to the display in order to generate the wave. Let's check the instructions for the next in display. Here we can use that function to send the values to the waveform. data ranges from zero to 255. Here is an example to send data I have created a function to send the sine wave to this display. Don't worry, I will explain this. But first let's define the object name here. This is the object's name for the waveform on the disk display here this function takes the parameters as the ID number which you can see here is one then the channel number two which you want to send the data to the amplitude of the sine wave, the frequency the Y shift and the grid height, which in my case is 40.

WNLOAD     DOCUMENT     SUPPORT     COMMUNITY     BLOG     CONTAC

- print/printh does not use Nextion Return Data, user must handle MCU side

usage: printh <hexhex>[<space><hexhex][...<space><hexhex]

<hexhex> is hexadecimal value of each nibble. 0x34 as 34

<space> is a space char 0x20, used to separate each <hexhex> pair

printh 0d // send single byte: value 13 hex: 0x0d

printh 0d 0a // send two bytes: value 13,10 hex: 0x0d0x0a

3       Add single value to Waveform Channel

- waveform channel data range is min 0, max 255

- 1 pixel column is used per data value added

- y placement is if value < s0.h then s0.y=s0.h-value, otherwise s0.y

usage: add <waveform>,<channel>,<value>

<waveform> is the .id of the waveform component

<channel> is the channel the data will be added to

<value> is ASCII text of data value, or numeric value

- valid: va0.val or sys0 or j0.val or 10

add 1,0,34 // add value 30 to Channel 0 of Waveform with .id 1

add 2,1,h0.val // add h0.val to Channel 1 of Waveform with .id 2

3    ● Add specified number of bytes to Waveform Channel over Serial from MCU

- waveform channel data range is min 0, max 255

- 1 pixel column is used per data value added.

- addt uses Transparent Data Mode (see 1.16)

- waveform will not refresh until Transparent Data Mode completes.

- qty limited by serial buffer (all commands+terminations + data < 1024)

- also refer to add command (see 3.19)

usage: add <waveform>,<channel>,<qty>

I have defined the number of samples as 100 Here, you can change them according to your requirement I will explain this part later. Let's come to the main part here I am using the sine function to get the value here. And this 127 is to keep the main position of the wave in the middle of the display as we saw the values ranges here from zero to 255 So that's why I am using 127 to bring the wave to the middle basically 127 will be added in each value of sine theta and therefore we will get the wave in the middle of the display also the Y shift will be added further to shift the wave up or down the display now we send the command with ID number channel number and the value and in the end, send the end command let's include the math dot h for sine function and stdio dot h for the S print F call the function in the while loop I have ID number one channel zero amplitude one frequency one know why shift and the grid height is 40 Let's build and flash this you can see the sine wave in the middle of the display this is because I haven't provided any why shift also the amplitude is one let's make some changes now I will first change the amplitude to two you can see the wave with amplitude of two let's increase frequency also this is working as expected I will change everything back to one and experiment with the shift in the Y axis. That small portion is cut from the display. Anyway, this is working just fine. Now coming to this grid calibration here. First we get the value of the grid width, which in my case is 40. But this function will get that value anyway And then we get the value for the grid height in this case, this value here will be neglected. Now, I have replaced the number of samples with the width and the rest of the functions are same.

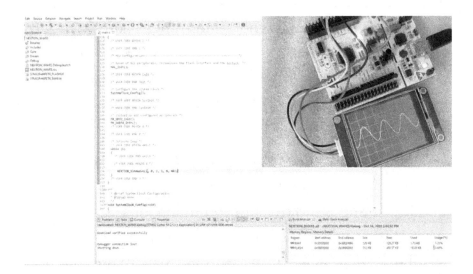

To use this part, we must define this in our code now you see this part is grayed out, let's build and flash you can see one oscillation of sine wave is equal to one with of the grid, I will change why shift back to zero and now you can see it perfectly, we can again change the amplitude and the frequency like we did earlier. That's all about the sine wave. I also want to include the square wave here this is exactly the same function as the sine wave except for this line here. This will basically limit the values to either high or low, no intermediate values let's call the square wave function also. Before that, I will disable the grid calibration. You can use this also I just want to use the simple one. Again, my ID number is one I want to use another channel for this and rest of the things are kept to default values this channel should be one as the first channel is zero. Let's build and flash you can see the square wave and the sine wave of same frequencies. Let's try to move the square wave a little upon the display I will change the y shift to two here and we got the perfect result. Obviously, one function is executing at a time and that's why the waves are shifting one at a time. If you want both of them to shift simultaneously, then send both the values for the sine wave and the square wave at the same time.

# EXAMPLE DUMMY CODE

Generating waveform patterns (sine wave and square wave) on a Nextion display using an STM32 microcontroller involves designing the waveform graphics in the Nextion Editor software and then controlling their display using the Nextion library in your microcontroller code. Below is a simplified example using an Arduino and the Nextion library.

Please note that you'll need to design the waveform graphics in the Nextion Editor and export the necessary files before proceeding with the code.

Design Waveform Graphics in Nextion Editor:

Create graphical components in the Nextion Editor to represent the waveform patterns (e.g., sine wave and square wave).
Export the Nextion project and obtain the .tft file.
Upload .tft File to Nextion Display:

Use the Nextion Editor's built-in upload tool to upload the .tft file to your Nextion display module.
Arduino Code Example:
Here's a simple Arduino code example that demonstrates how to control the display of waveform graphics on a Nextion display using the Nextion library.

Cpp

```cpp
#include <Nextion.h>

NexPicture pic_sine_wave = NexPicture(0, 1, "pic_sine_wave");  // Replace with your component's details
NexPicture pic_square_wave = NexPicture(0, 2, "pic_square_wave"); // Replace with your component's details
```

```
void setup() {
 Serial.begin(9600);
 nexInit(); // Initialize Nextion communication
}

void loop() {
 // Display sine wave
 pic_sine_wave.setPic(1); // Display the second
picture for sine wave

 // Wait for a while
 delay(2000); // Adjust delay time

 // Display square wave
 pic_square_wave.setPic(1); // Display the second
picture for square wave

 // Wait for a while
 delay(2000); // Adjust delay time
}
```

In this code, replace the pic_sine_wave and
pic_square_wave definitions with the appropriate
details of your components from the Nextion
Editor. The code switches between displaying the
sine wave and square wave graphics on the
Nextion display by using the setPic function.

Remember to adjust the code according to your specific Nextion display and the waveform graphics you've designed. Additionally, you might need to incorporate additional logic or animations based on your requirements.

Refer to the Nextion documentation, library, and your specific display's specifications for accurate details and usage instructions.

# GET STARTED WITH RIVERDI STM32 EMBEDDED DISPLAYS USING TOUCHGFX

Every display has its own advantages and disadvantages. Cheap displays are cheap, but it's very hard to program them and find a compatible library. HMI displays are a bit costlier and it's easier to interface them but most of them are missing a solid design or platform. Then the SD provides everything you need a decent display, a solid Designer software, and it comes with a price tag. But again, they don't provide higher resolution displays and also the form factor of the board is quite large. So a practical application is very hard. Today I have another display with me, which is manufactured by the company called reverdy. They are specialized in manufacturing different kinds of displays. And yes, it includes the one based on STM 32 MCU. Also, here you can check the STM 32 embedded displays. They generally provide the seven inch and 10.1 inch STM 32 based displays Rivoli has sent me one test unit, which is this one right here. It is a 10.1 inch TFT display with a resolution of 1280 by 800 pixels.

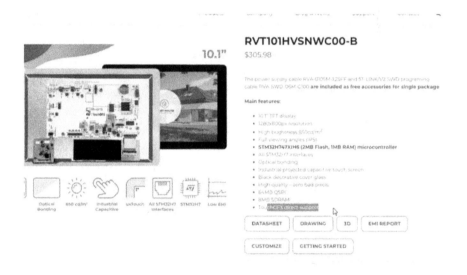

It is based on the STM 32x 747 MCU with two megabytes of internal flash and one megabyte of RAM. Other than that it also has the 64 megabytes of quad SPI and eight megabytes of SD RAM. And the best thing about this is that it has the official support from the touch GFX This is how the controller board at the back of the display looks like you can see it has the ports for different peripherals like F D can Rs 232 485 and one for the USB. This here is the power ports to power the display. It also has a Rebus connector to connect other Rebus displays manufactured by the reverdy. Here is the SWD port to debug the MCU water load the program into it. There is one expansion connector, which gives us access to other peripherals like I squared C, U, RT, SPI, PWM, ADC, et cetera. Before we go ahead with interfacing the display, let's see the unboxing first. Hello, my name is Camille, I'm CEO and founder of reverdy.

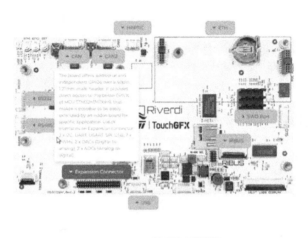

RS232

RS485

Fully independent 2xCAN FDx

Applicable in industrial and automotive area

And today we'll be unboxing our latest STM 32 embedded display in a size 10.1 inch, which is already available on our webshop and through our distribution network. So let's see, when you will buy a module from reberty on our distributors, you will buy it in a single package module like this one that I have here. And I will I'm going to show you what you will get inside what is included in the package and what is not included that you may need also to use this display. So first when you open the box you will see the package with the cables and the jumpers. So let me show you what we what we have here we have two cables. One is a power cable and one is a programming cable which is pretty important. So let's start first with the power cable. So we have a Molex five pin and in the second version of the display it will be six pin power connector, which on the both sides has a Molex connector, but in most cases, you will need to cut this cable and connect it to the power supply to connect the power to the display but the molex cable for the board is included and the second connector and the second cable we have here is a Molex to IDC connector, which is a programming cable and it's already prepared for Stelling programmer version two, which is the most common estate programmer right now on the market that is not included, of course into the display package, but you can use this cable connected directly to the SDM programmer, and then use this small MOLEX connector and connect to the board and start programming the display which will will show in another project how to start programming the display. Okay, so let's have a look into the box. What else do we have? Of course we will We'll find the display there. So let me take out this one and see what is in there. The display that I have here is the most sophisticated one it is equipped with a touchscreen that is optically bonded to the display so it's like fully equipped version so with the board with STM 30 287, microcontroller, all the memories, all the IOC connectors and the touchscreen that you can see here. So I have a display right now, then I will connect it because the display that you will receive from us is already of course tested and programmed with the demo application to show you how does it work. So here I have the cable that I already prepared with the power supply, I took a typical 12 volt power supply, but the power voltage on the connector is pretty wide. It's from six to 30 volts. So you can check this in detail in the datasheet of course, but I use the 12 volt which is very typical power supply that I have, I have a connector here and I will connect it right now. And what we should see is them application that I mentioned is already programmed. So as you see I already have it and of course then we can use the touchscreen as well. It's programmed and it's ready to play with so you can receive this display and immediately check its performance and of course the touch performance as well. So, this is all for today you know already and now and what to expect when you will buy a single module display from us with STM 32. So as I mentioned, you will have the power cable and you will have the programming cable in the box included. So your start with our display should be very fast and easy. Okay, so I wish you a fantastic projects with our displays. And please order them from our website or from our distributors network. Okay, thank you very much for today. Bye bye This is the back of the display. And here you can see the controller board. This here is the power port and this one is the SWD we have the USB port, the RS 485 and Rs 232. There are two can ports, a coin battery connector and the Rebus connector. You can also see the three buttons on the top left corner. The two buttons are user buttons and the third one is to reset the board. There is also a micro SD card connector. And lastly, we have the expansion connector to connect other devices or to use the I O pins. Let's see the documents provided by them for this display. We have the datasheet the drawing and a 3d view of file, there is an option to customize the order and a Getting Started page. In the customization page, you can customize the order as per your need. One important point I want to show here is that you can customize the cover glass even up to six millimeters and more so it allows us to use the display even outdoor. The Getting Started Guide focuses on touch GFX and how to program the display using it since that's what I am covering in this project. Let's close it for now. We will see the datasheet in a while.

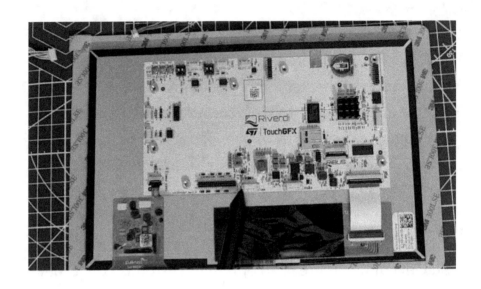

This 3d file I downloaded earlier I have AB viewer installed to see it this is how it looks in the AB viewer. Basically you can see the details of all the components used in the display. Well this could be extremely useful for designers and for mechanical engineers in the designing process. Let's check the datasheet now. Here you can see the naming convention of the display. This includes the company name, the display standard, the screen size resolution, et cetera. Here as per the electrical characteristics, the display can work with wide range of voltages typically ranging from 12 to 36 volts. I am using a 12 volt one amp pair adapter for it. All right now let's talk about the ports. First we have the power port. If you see here, the pins are numbered on the ports and below we have the details of the pins in the power port, we basically need to connect two pins, one for the power supply and another to the ground. This PIN number four can be used to enable or disable the power supply but by default this pin is enabled. If you want to turn off the display, you simply need to connect it to the ground. I am going to leave this pin open as it is anyway internally connected to the VDD. You can see the pin outs for other ports here. For now I am interested in SW D. Here you can see the connections for six pins and we need to connect them to the exact same pins on the SD link. Here you can see my power connector, I have only connected to pins one to the VCC and another to the ground. This is the connection to the SD link. Here I have connected all six pins to the respective pins on the SD link. And now we will simply connect the SD link to the SWD port and power connector to the power port. Next is the Rebus connector, just in case if you need to connect another display to it. Then comes the backlight setting. You can connect external display via the Rebus connector and select its backlight power source, it can be internal five volts or the main power supply. For details, please check the documentation. Here is the pin out for the expansion connector. And these are all the peripherals you can access with it. There are two user push buttons connected to PC six and PB zero. Also there is a user LED connected to P J 10. That is all the information there is in the datasheet. Let's start the touch GFX and design an application. I am going to design a simple application just to show you how to get started with it. For the rest, you can use all the touch GFX features as mentioned in my other projects, make sure you use the new version at least 4.20 onwards. here click on Create new and search reverdy You can click on the result and read about the display on the right this is the 10.1 inch display that I have. Let's give some name to the project and click Create. First of all I am going to add a background image. Here I already have a ping image of the same resolution. Let's add this image to the project. Next I am adding a slider and a gauge to this screen slider can have values from zero to 100. Configure the widgets as per your need.

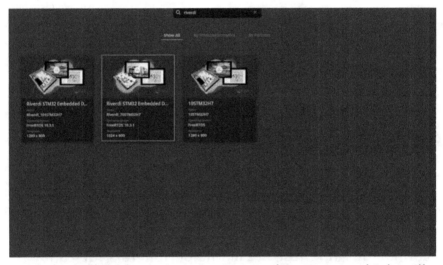

Now we will add one interaction to this screen which will be called when the slider value has changed. This will basically call a new function slider updated which we will later write in our IDE. The idea here is that the gauge should move as we change the slider. To do that we will write a small code in the IDE. The designing part is finished so generate the code. You can also run the simulator to see if everything is as per your design. Right now the slider is not changing because we haven't programmed it yet. Now go to the files. Here in the main prompt object folder, open the cube ID folder. Now open the project file in the cube ID. Alright, the project has been loaded, our entire project will be in the Cortex M seven. Here you can see the main dot c file. Notice that the script already initializes all the peripherals whether you use them or not, we are not working with the main file right now. So go to generated and open the screen one view base. Here you will see the function which we defined in the interaction, go to the definition of this function and copy it now go to the GUI folder and open the screen one view, we need to first define the function in the header file. So paste it here. Now we will call our function in the screen one view class. This will be basically called whenever the slider value changes. And here we will update the gauge with the same value. To do that, we will call the gauge dot set value and pass the value of the slider to it now invalidate the gauge so that new value can take effect. This is it. Let's build the code now. Let's first check in the simulator if it is working or not. You can see the gauge is updating as per the slider value, so we are good to go. Now comes the important part about how to load the program into the display. As per I have been told, there are two ways to do it. You cannot load it via the cube ID. You can directly load it via the touch GFX or use the cube programmer to do it. But even before that, we first need to copy the external loader into the cube program and directory. If you see here in the project structure, there is a s t LDR folder. It contains the external loader we need so open this folder and copy the loader. Now go to the directory where the cube programmer is installed. In my case it is in C program files SD Micro electronics STM 32, cube, STM 32 Cube programmer here go inside the bin and then external loader. Now paste the loader here. I already have it, so I will just replace that one. You just need to do it for the first project. Now I am going to load the project using the touch GFX but we need to restart it first or else it will not see the loader All right, let's load our project. I now click the Run target to load it to the display it takes a lot of time to build and load the project. All right, it's finally done. Now you have to press the reset button at the back to reset the display. Here we have our project. Let's see it in action you can see the gauge is responding according to the movement of the slider. The slider and gauge both are very responsive in their movement. So this is working very well. You only need to load the project once from the touch GFx. Let's say you modified the code and rebuilt the project loading it from touch GFX takes a lot of time. So now we will see how to load it via the cube programmer. Here you go to the debug folder. This file flash dot bin is generated whenever you build the project. So now we can just load this file and it will not take as much time as with the touch GFX open the cube programmer connects the st link. Now go to this download section. Make sure the addresses zero 8 million hexa. Browse the flash dot bin file we just saw. And click start programming to program the board. Remember that this will only load the code to the end ternal flash, so the queue SPI is unaffected from it. I just showed you a very simple application for this display. But as I said, you can use everything that I have covered in the touch GFX playlist. Now one very important thing you have to keep in mind, even though they provide the IOC file, it is not advised to generate the project from it. You can refer to it for the pin connections, but do not generate the project from it, or else it simply won't work. As I mentioned, in the beginning, the script they use pretty much initializes all the peripherals and components, so you just have to directly call the functions provided in the library. Like here is the SD card driver, and you already have the function like in it right blocks, re blocks etc. Or here you can see all the files for SD card, led buttons, Flash, et cetera. So you just have to analyze this project structure and use the functions provided to you. This is just like how St provides the examples in the repository.

Before we wrap up this project, let's see the demo project for this display. Go to touch GFX and create a new project select demos and click port specific demos. Here are the demos for the reverdy boards. Click Create to create the demo project here the demo project has been created now just run the target from here to load it on the display. Here you can see the project is running well on the display. So I hope you understood how to get started with the activity STM 32 based displays. The advantage you can have with it is that there already is a solid Designer software available for free and we already know the capabilities of using STM 32 as the controller you can purchase the display from reverdy website and there is no minimum order requirements so you can order even a single piece. The displays are also available in offer from the biggest distributors like Mouser the link to the website is in the description below.

# EXAMPLE DUMMY CODE

getting started with Riverdi STM32 embedded displays using TouchGFX involves setting up the hardware, creating a TouchGFX project, and writing code to interact with the display. Here's a general guide on how to get started:

Hardware Setup:

Connect your Riverdi STM32 embedded display to your STM32 microcontroller according to the display's datasheet and the microcontroller's pinout.
Ensure that the necessary power supply and communication interfaces (such as SPI) are properly connected.
Download TouchGFX:

Visit the TouchGFX website and download the TouchGFX Designer and the TouchGFX framework.
Create a TouchGFX Project:

Open the TouchGFX Designer.
Create a new project and select the display resolution and orientation that matches your Riverdi display.
Design the user interface using the TouchGFX

Designer's graphical interface.
Export Project to STM32CubeIDE:

Export the TouchGFX project to STM32CubeIDE.
This step generates the necessary C++ code and
assets for your user interface.
STM32CubeIDE Setup:

Open STM32CubeIDE and create a new project for
your STM32 microcontroller.
Configure the project settings and Clock settings
according to your hardware and requirements.
Integrate TouchGFX Code:

Copy the generated TouchGFX code (C++ files and
assets) from the exported project into your
STM32CubeIDE project.
Add any necessary libraries and configurations
required by your STM32 microcontroller.
Code Interaction:

In your application code, you can interact with the
TouchGFX UI elements.
Use TouchGFX-generated classes to control the UI,
update data, and respond to touch events.
Here's a simple example of how the main loop of
your STM32CubeIDE project might look, assuming
you have a button on the TouchGFX interface:

Cpp

```cpp
#include "main.h"
#include "TouchGFXGeneratedHAL.hpp"

int main(void) {
 HAL_Init();
 SystemClock_Config();
 MX_GPIO_Init();

 MX_TouchGFX_Init(); // Initialize TouchGFX

 while (1) {
  touchgfx::HAL::getInstance()->taskEntry();
  HAL_Delay(1);
 }
}
```

This example is a starting point, and you'll need to integrate your application's logic and UI updates based on your requirements.

Please refer to the specific documentation and resources provided by Riverdi, TouchGFX, and STM32CubeIDE for detailed step-by-step instructions, configuration details, and specific code examples relevant to your Riverdi display and

# INTERFACE BLDC MOTOR WITH STM32

This project will only cover the interfacing of those motors which are connected with the electronic speed controller or E SC. If you don't have the ESC and directly want to control the motor, this project is not for you BLDC motors can be controlled via the very similar process as we used to control the servo motor. I am going to use a potentiometer connected via the ADC to control the speed of the motor. We will see that but first let's see the connection. Here is my setup. I have the 30 ampere e SC, which is powered by a 12 volts adapter the ESC is connected to the 1400 KV motor, the two side pins can be connected to either side of the motor as it controls the direction of rotation, the center pin from the E s E should be connected to the center pin of the motor. Here the yellow wire is the center wire and the other two you can connect however you want. Three pin header cable from the ESC is responsible for controlling the speed of the motor. This is just like the three pin wire we see in a servo motor with red being the VCC brown being the ground and yellow is the signal pin the VCC and Ground have the potential difference of five volts. So you can use this to power the controller, I have connected them to the five volt pin on my f1 03 controller.

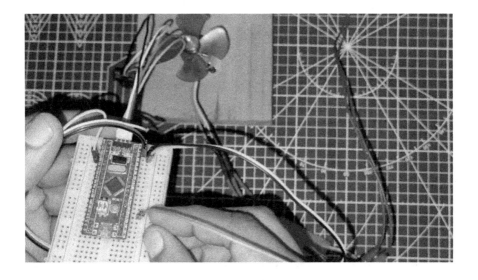

The signal pin is connected to the pin P A eight which I will set as the PWM output pin later, I have connected one potentiometer to the pin PA zero and this will be used to control the speed of the motor. This is it for the connection. Let's understand how this is going to work. As I mentioned, the BLDC can be controlled in the same way as the servo motor. I have already written a tutorial about the servo motor, so we will follow the same. As I mentioned here, we need a PWM signal of time period 20 milliseconds or a 50 hertz frequency, then the speed can be controlled by varying the pulse width between one millisecond to two milliseconds. That is all we need to do. Let's see how we can do this with the F 103 controller. Start the ID and create a new project. I am using the STM

32 F 103 C eight controller give some name to the project and click Finish. First of all I am selecting an external crystal to provide the clock. The board has eight megahertz crystal on it, and I want to run the system at maximum 72 megahertz. I am also using an ADC for the potentiometer and I want to keep the ADC clock to minimum. This is because I don't want the ADC to trigger the interrupts at a very high rate. I have already explained the ADC conversion time in another project. You can check that out. Anyway, this is the minimum I can set so let's go with it. Note that the APB two timer clock is at nine megahertz now, I am going to use the timer one for the PWM which is connected to the APB two bus. So the APB two timer clock is going to be the base clock for our timer. Select the debuggers serial wire and time basis sis tick. Let's configure the ADC first. I am using Channel Zero and remember that the potentiometer is connected to pin PA zero. I want the conversion to happen continuously so enable it.

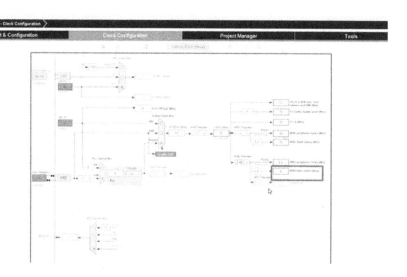

As I mentioned, I don't want the interrupts to trigger at a
very high rate. So I am selecting the maximum sampling
time. We will let the DMA handle these conversions.
Make sure to enable the circular mode. F 103 has a 12 bit
ADC so halfword is good enough. The DMA interrupt is
enabled so we are good to go. Now let's configure the
timer one. I am using channel one as the PWM
generation. Note here the pin PA eight is selected as the
PWM pin and this is where I have connected the signal pin
of the ESC timer one is connected to the APB two clock,
which is at nine megahertz right now. Now, let's
understand the calculations before we configure the
timer, we know the timers output frequency can be
calculated using this formula. Now if I want the output
frequency of 50 hertz, I can use the prescaler of 180. And
the auto reload of 1000. Using auto reload of 1000 is
better instead of 100. Because our pulse width is small,

and so does the duty cycle. With the reload value of 1000, we can accumulate more values for the duty cycle as compared to the value of 100. You will understand this in a while. So we know the minimum pulse width is going to be one millisecond, which is 5% of the 20 milliseconds, but our auto reload is at 1000. So a 5% Beauty means we have the value 50. So one millisecond is equivalent to the value 50. In our case, similarly two milliseconds will be equivalent to the value 100. Now since we have the auto reload of 1000, we could use the values from 50 to 100. But if we had 100, here, we could only use the values from five to 10. This is why I kept the auto reload at 1000 instead of 100. All right, let's set the values. The prescaler is 180 and auto reload is 1000. We will leave the rest of the setup to default. This pulse value will be changed during the runtime itself based on the input we get from the potentiometer. This is it for the Setup, click Save to generate the project. Let's write the code now. First, we will start the timer in PWM mode, I am using timer one channel one. Now start the ADC in the DMA mode, we will define the ADC data variable in a while and there is only one conversion to define the variable to store the ADC value. We need to convert the raw ADC value to our range of PWM values. So we will store the converted values in this variable. Now when the DMA will finish the conversion, the conversion completed callback will be called. Let's copy this definition. I am using the map function from the Arduino source code to map the ADC values to our range.

$$\text{Tim Freq} = \cfrac{A?B \text{ Clock}}{\left(\cfrac{ARR}{\uparrow}\right)\left(\cfrac{PS}{\uparrow}\right)}$$

$$= \cfrac{9000000}{1000 \times 180} = 50 \text{ Hz}$$

$$\frac{1 \text{ ms}}{20 \text{ ms}} = 5\% \text{ duty}$$

$$\text{Duty} = \frac{\text{Value}}{ARR} = \frac{50}{1000} = 5\%.$$

$1 \text{ ms} \longrightarrow 50$

$2 \text{ ms} \longrightarrow 100$

The values will be stored in the converted variable, we want to map the ADC data variable value, the minimum value of this variable can be zero, and the maximum can be 4095. Since it's a 12 bit ADC value, the minimum output value can be 50 and the maximum can be 100. This is as per the duty cycle we calculated earlier. So basically, when the potentiometer reads zero, this function will output 50. And when the potentiometer is at maximum 4095 This function will output 100. Now we need to send these values to our timer so that the duty cycle can be varied. I am using timer one channel one so the CCR one that is capture compare register one, you can use another capture compare register if you are using another channel of your timer. If you are familiar with

BLDC motors, you might know that we also need to calibrate the ESC this code will do that for you. Basically, we set the maximum duty that is the pulse of two milliseconds and wait for some time. The e s c will sound the beep indicating it has been calibrated for the high pulse. Now send the lowest duty that is the pulse of one millisecond and again wait for some time. The e s c will again sound the beep indicating it has been calibrated for the low pulse. I have defined this at the top of the file so that you can enable this only if you want to calibrate all right, let's build the code the start DMA function takes a 32 bit variable. So let me typecast this all right Everything is set. Now, let's debug the code. I will use the motor later. First we will see the results in the debugger and the logic analyzer, we will monitor the ADC converted variable. Here the potentiometer is at zero, so the value is 50. And if I move the potentiometer to maximum, the value has been increased to 100. Let's see the pulse timing on in the logic analyzer. I have connected the pin P ah to the Channel Zero of the analyzer. Here you can see the pulse remains high for one millisecond out of 20 milliseconds period. And now I am rotating the potentiometer to the maximum position. Now we have the pulse width the width of two milliseconds. Here the value of the variable is 100.

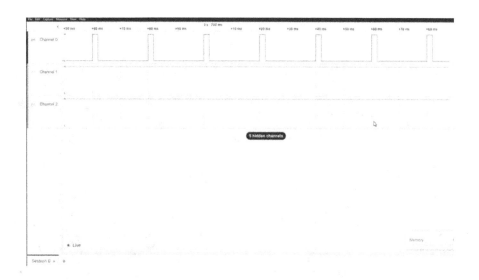

So the pulse timing is correct. Let's switch on the motor. I will disconnect the controller so that it will directly get the power from the ESC itself you can hear the set of beats produced by the ESC it means the calibration is completed. Let's rotate the motor you can judge the speed by listening to the sound it is making. So the motor is rotating fine, and we were able to control it using the potentiometer. If you don't want to do the calibration, just set this definition to zero and this particular code will be excluded. This is it for the project. I hope you understood how we can control the BLDC motor using the STM 32.

# EXAMPLE DUMMY CODE

Interfacing a BLDC (Brushless Direct Current) motor with an STM32 microcontroller involves using motor driver hardware to control the motor's speed and direction. Here's a basic example using an STM32 microcontroller and a BLDC motor driver like the popular DRV8302.

Please note that BLDC motor control can be complex and requires a deep understanding of motor driver ICs, PWM, and feedback mechanisms. This example provides a simplified overview and might need further adjustments according to your specific motor and driver.

Hardware Setup:

Connect your BLDC motor to the motor driver (e.g., DRV8302).
Connect the motor driver's control pins (e.g., PWM, direction) to STM32 GPIO pins.
Connect the motor driver's current sensing outputs (if applicable) to ADC pins for feedback.
STM32CubeIDE Setup:

Create a new STM32CubeIDE project for your STM32 microcontroller.

Configure GPIO pins for PWM control and direction.
Configure ADC pins for current sensing feedback (if applicable).
PWM Control and Motor Direction:

Configure a PWM timer to generate PWM signals for controlling the motor speed.
Use GPIO pins to control the motor direction.
Current Sensing (Optional):

Configure ADC channels to read the current sensing feedback signals from the motor driver.
Use ADC readings to implement current-based control algorithms.
Here's a simplified example of how your code might look to control a BLDC motor using an STM32 and a DRV8302 driver:

C

```c
#include "stm32f4xx_hal.h"

// Define PWM timer and channels
TIM_HandleTypeDef htim1;
TIM_OC_InitTypeDef sConfigOC;

// Define GPIO pins for motor direction
```

```c
#define MOTOR_DIRECTION_PIN GPIO_PIN_0
#define MOTOR_DIRECTION_PORT GPIOA

// Define PWM period (adjust according to your
motor's requirements)
#define PWM_PERIOD 1000

void SystemClock_Config(void);
static void MX_GPIO_Init(void);
static void MX_TIM1_Init(void);

int main(void) {
 HAL_Init();
 SystemClock_Config();
 MX_GPIO_Init();
 MX_TIM1_Init();

 HAL_TIM_PWM_Start(&htim1, TIM_CHANNEL_1);

 while (1) {
  // Control motor direction
  HAL_GPIO_WritePin(MOTOR_DIRECTION_PORT,
MOTOR_DIRECTION_PIN, GPIO_PIN_SET);

  // Adjust PWM duty cycle to control motor speed
  __HAL_TIM_SET_COMPARE(&htim1,
TIM_CHANNEL_1, 500); // Adjust duty cycle
```

```
    // Implement feedback control (if applicable)
    // Read ADC values for current sensing
    // Implement control algorithms based on current
feedback
  }
}

void SystemClock_Config(void) {
  // Configure the system clock as needed
}

static void MX_GPIO_Init(void) {
  // Initialize GPIO pins for motor direction
  GPIO_InitTypeDef GPIO_InitStruct = {0};
  __HAL_RCC_GPIOA_CLK_ENABLE();
  HAL_GPIO_WritePin(MOTOR_DIRECTION_PORT,
MOTOR_DIRECTION_PIN, GPIO_PIN_RESET);
  GPIO_InitStruct.Pin = MOTOR_DIRECTION_PIN;
  GPIO_InitStruct.Mode =
GPIO_MODE_OUTPUT_PP;
  GPIO_InitStruct.Pull = GPIO_NOPULL;
  GPIO_InitStruct.Speed = GPIO_SPEED_FREQ_LOW;
  HAL_GPIO_Init(MOTOR_DIRECTION_PORT,
&GPIO_InitStruct);
}

static void MX_TIM1_Init(void) {
  // Initialize PWM timer and channel
```

```
htim1.Instance = TIM1;
htim1.Init.Prescaler = 0;
htim1.Init.CounterMode =
TIM_COUNTERMODE_UP;
htim1.Init.Period = PWM_PERIOD;
htim1.Init.ClockDivision =
TIM_CLOCKDIVISION_DIV1;
HAL_TIM_PWM_Init(&htim1);

sConfigOC.OCMode = TIM_OCMODE_PWM1;
sConfigOC.Pulse = 0;
sConfigOC.OCPolarity = TIM_OCPOLARITY_HIGH;
sConfigOC.OCFastMode = TIM_OCFAST_DISABLE;
HAL_TIM_PWM_ConfigChannel(&htim1,
&sConfigOC, TIM_CHANNEL_1);
}
```

Please note that BLDC motor control often requires advanced algorithms, such as field-oriented control (FOC), sensorless control, and current feedback loops. This example provides a basic starting point, but you'll likely need to delve deeper into motor control techniques for more complex applications.

Always consult the datasheets of your microcontroller, motor driver, and other components for accurate details and refer to the

# INTERFACE RS485 MODULE WITH STM32

I am going to use the RS 485 for the Modbus Communication and this is why today's project is kind of related to Modbus also, today we will see how to use the RS 485 to TTL converter with our microcontroller.

| Specifications | RS232 | RS485 |
|---|---|---|
| Mode of Operation | Single ended | Differential |
| No. of drivers and receivers | 1 driver, 1 receiver | 32 drivers, 32 receivers |
| Max. cable length | 50 ft | 4000 ft |
| Data rate | 20kb/s | 10Mb/s |
| Driver output voltage | +/-25V | -7V to +12V |
| Signal level(Loaded min) | +/-5V to +/-15V | +/-1.5 V |
| Signal level (Unloaded Max) | +/-25V | +/-6V |
| Driver load impedance | 3k to 7k | 54 |
| Receiver input V range | +/-15V | -7 to +12V |
| Receiver input sensitivity | +/-3V | +/-200mV |

So what is this Rs 485. To put it in simple words, just like Rs 232 Rs 485 as a protocol for serial communication. Compared to Rs 232. It is faster and can be used for data transmission over longer cable lengths and in noisy environments. Since the STM 32 microcontrollers do not support the RS 485 communication, we will use the RS 485 to TTL converter. This converter uses the max 485 Chip and converts the TTL signals to Rs 485 and vice versa. The converter has pins A and B here a is the non inverting pin and B is the inverting pin. Say for example, if the chip is powered with five volts, and we are sending zero cross nine five via the UART the max 485 chip will amplify each bit and this is how the output on the pins A and B is going to look like notice that pin A is a non inverting pin. So the signal on it is either zero or plus five volts. On the other hand, pin B is an inverting pin. So the signal is either zero or minus five volts.

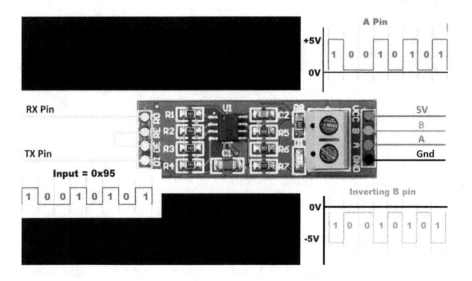

Now when this data is received by another module, it will interpret a zero or one based on these differences. If the voltage differences maximum between the pins, it's a one and if the difference is zero, the bid is also zero. I hope you understood how communication works. Now let's talk about the connection. This is how the connection looks overall I have two MC use which are connected via the two Rs 485 to TTL converters. Let's dig deep into this. This picture shows the pin out of the module on the right side we have the VCC ground pin A and pin V the pins A and B must be connected to the similar pins on the other module, you can see the connections between the corresponding A and B pins. I have already explained the purpose of these pins on the left side the pin R O which stands for receiver output must be connected to the RX pin of the MCU the pin D i driver input is connected to the TX pin of the MCU the pins are E and D are connected together R E stands for receiver enable it enables the module to receive the data but this is a low enable that means we must pull a pin low in order to enable the receiver similar similarly D which is driver enable enables the module to transmit the data. Since this is a high enable pin, we must pull it high in order to enable the transmit mode. So in order to transmit the data that a pin must be pulled high and the ar e pin also should be high. Similarly to receive the data the R E pin must be pulled low and D pin also should be low. This is why both the pins are tied together. So pulling either one of them will also pull another pin to the same state. This is the connection between the MCU and the module.

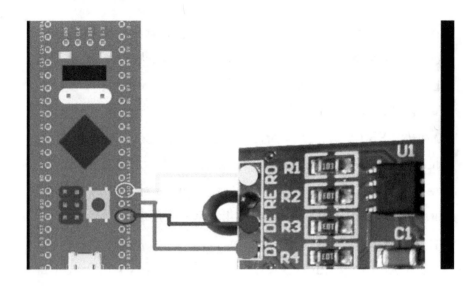

The arm open is connected to the PA 10 the UART one Rx pin the DI pin is connected to the PA nine the UART one Tx pin and T E and R E are connected to the pin P A eight which we will set as the output later. The connection will remain similar with the other MCU also Let's start the Q ID and create a new project. I am using the STM 32 F 103 controller, give some name to the project and click Finish. First of all we will enable the external crystal for the clock. The board has eight megahertz crystal on it and we will run it at maximum 72 megahertz then go to sis debug and enable serial wire set the time based source to cystic also now go to connectivity UART one and enable the asynchronous mode. You can see here the pins p a 10 and P A nine are enabled as the RX and TX pins. Let's keep the baud rate at 11 Five 200 We have eight bit word length, no parity and one stop bit. Let's go to the interrupt tab and enable the UART interrupt. We will use the interrupt to receive data from the module. This is it for the UART now we will set the pin PA eight as the output pin. This is where the R E and D pins will be connected. I am naming this pin as the TX enable pin, click Save to generate the code. Let's first create the TX and RX buffers. Inside the main function, we will call the receive to idle function in interrupt mode. If you have been watching this channel, you know what this function does for the rest of you guys, I will leave the link to the project in the description below. Basically during receiving if the UART sees the line idle for some time, it triggers the interrupt. This interrupt eventually calls the RX event handler function. We will copy this event handle in our main file, and inside it we will restart the interrupt hold disables the interrupt after one call, so we need to enable it again. Now we need to send the data to the UART so that it can be transferred via the module. Let's first create an index variable, we will continuously transfer the data in the while loop. First, we will copy this string to the TX data array. This string will always have the updated value of the index variable, then we will call the function send data to send this string to the UART. We will define this function later.

```
100
101     HAL_UARTEx_ReceiveToIdle_IT(&huart1, RxData, 16);
102
103     /* USER CODE END 2 */
104
105     /* Infinite loop */
106     /* USER CODE BEGIN WHILE */
107     while (1)
108     {
109         /* USER CODE END WHILE */
110
111         /* USER CODE BEGIN 3 */
112
113         sprintf
114     }
115     /* USER CODE END 3 */
116  }
117
118 /**
119   * @brief System Clock Configuration
120   * @retval None
121   */
122 void SystemClock_Config(void)
123 {
124     RCC_OscInitTypeDef RCC_OscInitStruct = {0};
```

F103_RS485_TUT
> Includes
> Core
> Drivers
  F103_RS485_TUT.ioc
  STM32F103C8TX_FLASH.ld

And this process will repeat every one second. Now let's define the send data function. As I mentioned in the beginning, the R E and D pins set the module as receiver or transmitter. Before sending the data, we need to set this module as a transmitter. And to do that we have to pull the D pin as high. So here first of all, we will set the TX enable pin as high then we will transmit the data via the UART. And again, we will pull the pin low so as to enable the receiver mode. Basically, the module is always in the receiver mode, because we don't know when the data might arrive. Just before we send the data, we put it in the transmitter mode and after sending it goes back to the receiver mode again, we need to include some header files for the S printf and the string length functions all right, everything is fine. Now, I am using a 446 r e as the second controller which is connected to another module. The code used is exactly similar to the first one here is the send data function. In the first controller I am sending the string which starts with F 103. When the data is received by the second controller, it will just modify the first four bytes to a 446 and send the same string back to the first controller. Since I want this second controller to only respond to the data sent by the first one, this is why the transmission program is written in the callback itself. There is nothing inside the while loop here. The code is already loaded into the F 446. So we will just see the f1 03 debugger. All right, let's test this now. both the controllers are connected to the same computer. So I am fixing the st link to this configuration. Here I have put both the buffers in the live expression. Let's put a breakpoint at the send data function. Here you can see the data stored in the TX buffer. And now this data will be sent to the module. Let's put another breakpoint in the callback function. It didn't hit the breakpoint, but it's fine. Here you can see the data received. We have some garbage characters also. But this is because I didn't reset the F 446. And it already had the data in the RX buffer. Just ignore it. For now. The data is exactly what we sent, but the 103 has been replaced with 446.

We have hit the breakpoint this time, but the received data is the same. Let me try again. Seems like the received data is not updating, maybe because of the breakpoints. Let's remove them and run the code freely. All right, now you can see the received data is exactly the same that we are sending except for the first few bytes. Anyway, you can clear the buffer in the second controller after sending the data that way it will not send the extra characters. That's all for this project. In the next project, we will start with the Modbus and obviously we will use this Rs 485 module with it. We will use STM 32 as the master and read some holding and input registers of the slave.

# EXAMPLE DUMMY CODE

here's a basic example of how you can interface an RS485 module with an STM32 microcontroller using HAL (Hardware Abstraction Layer) libraries. RS485 is a differential communication protocol commonly used for long-range communication.

In this example, I'll assume you have a specific RS485 module with its UART connections and appropriate driver chips (such as MAX485) already connected to your STM32 microcontroller.

C

```c
#include "main.h"
#include "stm32f4xx_hal.h"

UART_HandleTypeDef huart2; // UART2 is used in this example

void SystemClock_Config(void);
static void MX_GPIO_Init(void);
static void MX_USART2_UART_Init(void);

int main(void) {
 HAL_Init();
 SystemClock_Config();
```

```c
MX_GPIO_Init();
MX_USART2_UART_Init();

uint8_t txData[] = "Hello from STM32!";
uint8_t rxData[50];

while (1) {
 HAL_UART_Transmit(&huart2, txData,
sizeof(txData), HAL_MAX_DELAY);
 HAL_Delay(1000);

 HAL_UART_Receive(&huart2, rxData,
sizeof(rxData), HAL_MAX_DELAY);
 // Process received data (if needed)
 }
}

void SystemClock_Config(void) {
 // Configure the system clock as needed
}

static void MX_GPIO_Init(void) {
 // Initialize GPIO pins as needed
}

static void MX_USART2_UART_Init(void) {
 huart2.Instance = USART2;
 huart2.Init.BaudRate = 9600;
```

```
 huart2.Init.WordLength =
UART_WORDLENGTH_8B;
 huart2.Init.StopBits = UART_STOPBITS_1;
 huart2.Init.Parity = UART_PARITY_NONE;
 huart2.Init.Mode = UART_MODE_TX_RX;
 huart2.Init.HwFlowCtl =
UART_HWCONTROL_NONE;
 HAL_UART_Init(&huart2);
}
```

In this code, HAL_UART_Transmit is used to send data via RS485 and HAL_UART_Receive is used to receive data. Replace USART2 with the appropriate UART instance for your specific STM32 microcontroller. Make sure you've properly configured the UART pins and other settings in STM32CubeMX before using this code.

Remember to adapt the code according to your hardware configuration, STM32 series, and specific requirements. Additionally, you may need to implement RS485-specific features like control of the driver enable (DE) and receiver enable (RE) pins based on your module's design.

# FLASH DRIVE WITH STM32 USB HOST MSC CUBEIDE

I will show you how to use STM 32 as a host for the mass storage class. This means you can connect your flash drive to it and read and write some files or folders in the flash drive. Let's start by creating a project in cube ID. This time I am using STM 32 F four Discovery Board give some name to this project and click finish here we are in our cube MX opened the user manual for your board it will come handy soon let's clear the pin outs first.

I am enabling the external crystal for the clock let's select the UART for the debugging purpose 9600 baud rate is just a choice you can select any other to now click USB OTG F s and select host only make sure you enable the V bus because flash drives don't have any external power supply. So we need to power them via V bus. As you can see two data pins and one V bus pin got selected. Now go to USB host and select USB Mass Storage Class click yes we will leave everything default here now let's enable the FAT file system. We will enable the USB disk as we are interfacing USB. Here we need to make some changes. Enable the long file names. Select the static buffer on VSS. Here you can change the maximum length of the file names. Select the maximum sector size to max possible. If you want to enable the exFAT support enable it here there is one very important piece of information about the V bus that I missed. Go to USB host platform settings. As you can see here, there is no solution for V bus. This is because V bus power must be turned on and the macu have a pin connection for that you will understand it better when we take a look at the user manual for this discovery board. Here is the diagram that we need. This right here is our micro usb as you can see the V bus is being powered from PCs zero pin. PC zero is connected to enable pin which is an active low pin. This means in order to turn it on, we need to give a lowered PC zero which will turn on the power supply for the V bus select the PCs zeros output. In the GP i o settings make sure that it's slow. Click Save to generate the code Also note that the V bus GP i o have a solution now, and that's p c zero.

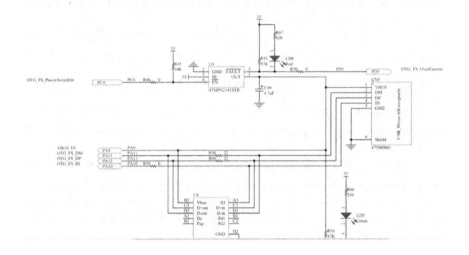

This is it for the setup. Let's go to our program window. Here is the main dot c file. Let's first include the libraries put the file handling dot c file in the source folder and file handling dot h file in the include folder let's refresh the project so that we can see them you can change your controller header here. Here you can change the UART File Handling is exactly the same file that we used while interfacing the SD card I just made some changes like brought the USB path here. Other than this there are some changes in the names of different locations and that's pretty much all all the functions are same as they were in the SD card handling now let's go to the file where we need to make changes that is USB host dot c file. First let's include the file handling here scroll down to USB H use of process. Here we have all the cases like what to do when the USB connects or disconnects or when it is ready for communication we are going to write once the

USB is ready for communication. First of all, mount the USB check the USB details about total and free space this will list all the directories and files in the USB drive you can see we have all these functions available for USB let's create a file in the root folder and we will call it root file dot txt write some data to this file now I am creating a directory in the root folder and its name is directory one create a file inside this directory write some data to this file now. The first parameter of right file is the name of the file that you want to write.

And the second parameter is the data creating another directory inside the root folder I am creating yet another directory inside the directory to and create a file inside sub directory. Now write some data to this file we can also update the files. Here I am updating the route file itself. When we wrote the data to route file in the beginning there was a line break so this data must be in the second line. This is all for files and directories. Know when the USB is disconnected we will call the unmount function let's build this and flash to our board. First of all I will format the USB so that there are no files and folders present before writing. Let's insert the USB now I will format it first. If you remembered I did enable the exFAT support, so I can format it in exFAT file system it's completed there is nothing inside the USB the serial window here is for keeping the trace of what's happening Okay, let's run the code now connect your USB and you can see the output on the console you can pause the project and read them. Basically, all the operations are completed successfully. I have removed the USB now.

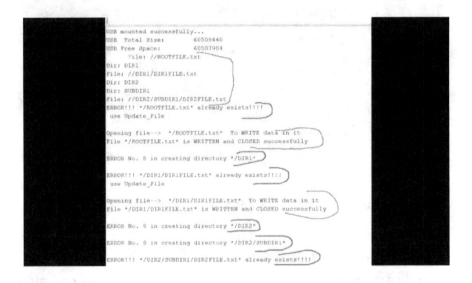

```
USB mounted successfully...
USB  Total Size:        60509440
USB  Free Space:        60507904
          File: //ROOTFILE.txt
Dir: DIR1
File: //DIR1/DIR1FILE.txt
Dir: DIR2
Dir: SUBDIR1
File: //DIR2/SUBDIR1/DIR2FILE.txt
ERROR!!! */ROOTFILE.txt* already exists!!!!
 use Update_File

Opening file--> */ROOTFILE.txt*  To WRITE data in it
File */ROOTFILE.txt* is WRITTEN and CLOSED successfully

ERROR No. 8 in creating directory */DIR1*

ERROR!!! */DIR1/DIR1FILE.txt* already exists!!!!
 use Update_File

Opening file--> */DIR1/DIR1FILE.txt*  To WRITE data in it
File */DIR1/DIR1FILE.txt* is WRITTEN and CLOSED successfully

ERROR No. 8 in creating directory */DIR2*

ERROR No. 9 in creating directory */DIR2/SUBDIR1*

ERROR!!! */DIR2/SUBDIR1/DIR2FILE.txt* already exists!!!!
```

And you can see the unmounting also got executed. Let's see the files on the computer now. So we have two directories and a route file, just like we created data is also in the correct position sub directories present inside the directory to he'd also have exactly the same text that we wrote in it. Route file have both the initial data and the updated data also. If you insert the USB again, you will see something like this on the serial console. Here it shows all the files and directories present on the flash drive. It is represented by the first green line. Now, as these files are already present, new ones can't be created. And that's why there is error and you can see them in the red color. When we write the data to these files, the old data will be overwritten and the right will be successful. And you can see the green color in between representing this scenario. I have plans for USB H ID for keyboard and mouse and I will make the project on it very soon.

## EXAMPLE DUMMY CODE

here's an example code for using the STM32 USB Host MSC (Mass Storage Class) to interface with a USB flash drive using STM32CubeIDE. The example demonstrates how to detect and interact with a USB flash drive connected to the STM32 microcontroller.

Please note that you need to have the necessary

hardware and a USB Host library supporting MSC (Mass Storage Class) enabled in your STM32CubeIDE project.

Create a New Project:

Open STM32CubeIDE and create a new project for your STM32 microcontroller.
Configure the Clock settings and other necessary configurations.
Configure USB Host MSC:

Open the "USB_HOST" configuration in STM32CubeMX.
Enable the "MSC (Mass Storage Class)" middleware.
Configure the necessary pins and settings for USB Host communication.
Generate Code:

Generate the code using STM32CubeMX.
USB Host MSC Example Code:
Here's a basic example code that demonstrates detecting and interacting with a USB flash drive using the USB Host MSC library in STM32CubeIDE.

C

```c
#include "usb_host.h"

USBH_HandleTypeDef hUSB_Host;

void SystemClock_Config(void);

int main(void) {
 HAL_Init();
 SystemClock_Config();

 USBH_Init(&hUSB_Host, USBH_UserProcess, 0);
 USBH_RegisterClass(&hUSB_Host,
USBH_MSC_CLASS);

 while (1) {
  USBH_Process(&hUSB_Host);
 }
}

void SystemClock_Config(void) {
 // Configure the system clock as needed
}

void USBH_UserProcess(USBH_HandleTypeDef
*phost, uint8_t id) {
 switch (id) {
  case HOST_USER_SELECT_CONFIGURATION:
   break;
```

```
  case HOST_USER_DISCONNECTION:
  // Handle disconnection event
  break;
 case HOST_USER_CLASS_ACTIVE:
  // USB flash drive detected and ready
  // You can use USBH_MSC_BOT_Init() and
USBH_MSC_Read/Write functions
  break;
 case HOST_USER_CONNECTION:
  // Handle USB flash drive connection
  break;
 default:
  break;
 }
}
```

In this example, the USBH_UserProcess function handles various events like USB device connection, disconnection, and configuration selection. You can add code to read/write data to the USB flash drive once it's detected and ready.

Please refer to the specific STM32CubeIDE documentation and USB Host MSC library documentation for detailed step-by-step instructions, configuration details, and specific code examples relevant to your STM32 series and the USB Host MSC implementation.

# HC12 WITH STM32 F446 F103 2 WAY COMMUNICATION

We will see how to use h c 12 wireless transceiver with STM 32 I will first cover how to set up H C 12 for communication and later I will use STM 32 to do the communication between them.

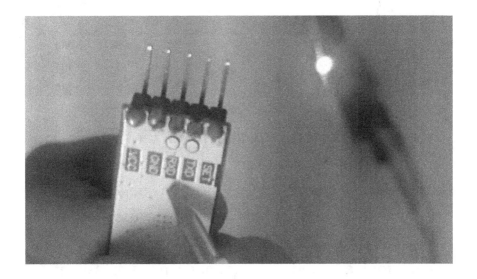

So, let's start with the setup first here is the h c 12 I am going to use I have one more obviously and it looks like this. If you compare them side by side you can see the difference Yes, I got a fake one but unintended Of course, there is crucial difference between both the range is an issue for the fake hc 12 But we can fix it and I will leave the link for the fix in the description I have already fixed the range so I am going to use it as you can see at the back here we have Vcc ground RX Tx and the set pin so I am connecting ground to ground five volts to Vcc TX to RX and RX to Tx.

Meanwhile, when the module is set to be FU2 mode in FU1 and FU3 mode, the baud rate exceeding 4,800bps will be automatically reduced to be 4,800bps. In FU2 mode, the sending time interval of data package cannot be too short, otherwise, the data will be lost. It is suggested that the sending time interval of data package should not be less than 1 sec.

The following gives some characteristics reference values of various modes:

| Mode | FU1 | FU2 | FU3 | Remark |
|---|---|---|---|---|
| Idle current | 3.6mA | 80μA | 16mA | Average value |
| Transmission time delay | 15-25mS | 500mS | 4-80mS | Sending one byte |
| Loopback test time delay 1 | 31mS | | | Serial port baud rate 9,600, sending one byte |
| Loopback test time delay 2 | 31mS | | | Serial port baud rate 9,600, sending ten bytes |

Note: Loopback test time delay means the duration from the time of, after conducting short circuit on TX and RX pins of one module and sending serial port data to the other module, starting to send serial port data to the other module to the time that the returned data appear at TX pin of the other module.

**Module Parameter Setting AT Command**
AT command is used to set the module parameters and switch the module functions, and after setting, it will be valid only after exiting from setting state. Meanwhile, modification of parameters and functions will not be lost in case of power failure.

(1) Command mode entering
The first way to enter: in normal use (energized), put Pin 5 "SET" in low level.
The second way to enter: disconnect power supply, first put Pin 5 "Set" in low level,

Now the set pin must be pulled low for the AT commands. So connect that to the ground I have connected it to the FTDI serial device and you can see in the device manager the Comm port is four so let's open the console of Comm four choose the baud rate of 9600. This 9600 baud rate is default for h c 12 and it is mentioned in the datasheet. Let's open the connection type the A T and send you can see the response from the H C 12. Let's see what other commands that we can use here this is to change the baud rate to change the communication channel A t plus r is used for inquiry let's inquire the channel I think it's uppercase C yes the communication channel is set to one Ward rate is set to 9600 you can type a t plus r x to inquire about all the parameters of once you can see the details in the datasheet the transmitting power is set to max and the mode is fu three I am leaving everything to default as this is the best setup you can change them according to your requirement now let's create the project in cube ID.

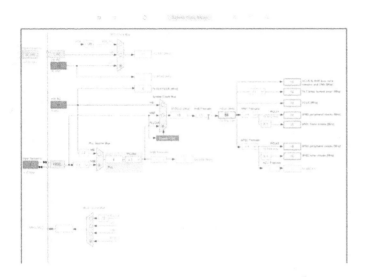

I am going to use both STM 32 F 446 and F 103 for connecting each H C 12. First I am creating the project for f 446. Give some name and click Finish. Here is the cube MX select External crystal for the clock now you want one is where the device will be connected. Turn on the interrupt If you want to use the ring buffer here use the baud rate of 9600. You R two is for communicating with the computer same setup is required here too now the clock setup I have eight megahertz Crystal and I want the system to run at maximum clock click Save to generate the project here is our main file here I am going to send some data to the HC 12. And I want the process to repeat every two seconds let's build it we have no errors. So let's go ahead and flash this as I am connecting two different MC use to the same computer I will face some issues with the SD link. To avoid that connect the first SD link only.

Now in the debug configuration, select the SD link serial number and tap on scan as there is only one st link connected it will show up and now this particular project will only use this particular st link the code is successfully flashed This is it for the transmitter. Now I am going to create another project for the receiver here I am using F 103 C eight MCU and the rest of the setup will remain exactly the same. Here in the main file, create an array to store the received data now how you receive will receive 22 bytes of data in the blocking mode and then transmits the data to the computer let's build it and flash now I am connecting the second st link. Check the serial number again and Tap Scan. You can see both the SD links are being detected. As I already know that this one is the first one so select the second and click Apply. Now this project will always use the second st link regardless of how many are connected. So we have flushed both transmitter and receiver. Let's see the connection once. This wire right here is connected between the RX pin of the HC 12 and the UART one TX This one is connected between the TX Of The HC 12 and the UART. One RX VCC is connected to five volts from the MCU and note that the set pin is not connected anywhere we need to leave it like that for communication. And while using the 80 commands ground the set pin the similar connection is in the receiver and also TX to RX and RX to Tx. Also I have connected the UART two pins to the FTDI to communicate with the computer let's open the console and set the comport for the receiver as you can see the data is receiving every two seconds as we expect it. I have tested this for a pretty good range and it works as stated. Obviously I couldn't test for two kilometers range but I think it should work for a fairly large range too. Now let's move to the more complex part. And here we will do a two way communication between both the HC 12 modules. To do so, I will use my UAF ring buffer library I already have a project on it you can check on the top right corner let's include the library files put the C file in the source directory and header file in the include directory do the same for the second project also let's modify the F 103 project first include the UART ring buffer dot h file change the header file according to your controller now we need to copy this and paste it in the interrupt file and change the default interrupt handler to the modified one. Now in the main file, first define the device UART and PC UART.

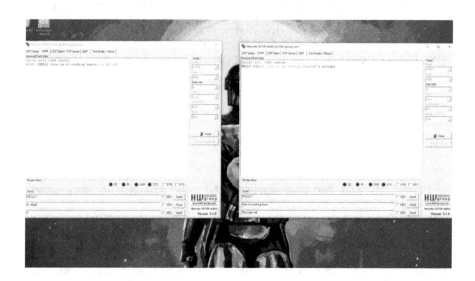

In the main function call the ring buffer initialization function and now if the data is available from PC it will read it and send it to the device and if the data is available from device it will read it and send it to the computer that's all now let's build it we need to do the same steps in the second projectile so I will just fast forward this part let's build it and flashed to the MCU flash the first one also so we are all set now let's open another instance of this console. So one is at Comm port three and another at comport four here the pink color is the one I am sending and black color is the one receiving you can see the communication is working both ways. And as this is using ring buffer we can send random number of characters also.

# EXAMPLE DUMMY CODE

here's a basic example of how you can establish two-way communication between two STM32 microcontrollers (STM32F446 and STM32F103) using HC-12 wireless modules. The HC-12 modules use serial communication to transmit and receive data wirelessly.

Please note that you need to have the necessary HC-12 modules and UART (serial) communication configured on both STM32 microcontrollers.

STM32F446 Code (Transmitter):

C

```
#include "main.h"
#include "stm32f4xx_hal.h"

UART_HandleTypeDef huart2;

void SystemClock_Config(void);
static void MX_GPIO_Init(void);
static void MX_USART2_UART_Init(void);
```

```c
int main(void) {
 HAL_Init();
 SystemClock_Config();
 MX_GPIO_Init();
 MX_USART2_UART_Init();

 char txData[] = "Hello from STM32F446!";

 while (1) {
  HAL_UART_Transmit(&huart2, (uint8_t*)txData,
strlen(txData), HAL_MAX_DELAY);
  HAL_Delay(1000);
 }
}

void SystemClock_Config(void) {
 // Configure the system clock as needed
}

static void MX_GPIO_Init(void) {
 // Initialize GPIO pins as needed
}

static void MX_USART2_UART_Init(void) {
 huart2.Instance = USART2;
 huart2.Init.BaudRate = 9600;
 huart2.Init.WordLength =
```

```c
UART_WORDLENGTH_8B;
 huart2.Init.StopBits = UART_STOPBITS_1;
 huart2.Init.Parity = UART_PARITY_NONE;
 huart2.Init.Mode = UART_MODE_TX;
 huart2.Init.HwFlowCtl =
UART_HWCONTROL_NONE;
 HAL_UART_Init(&huart2);
}
```

STM32F103 Code (Receiver):

C

```c
#include "main.h"
#include "stm32f1xx_hal.h"

UART_HandleTypeDef huart1;

void SystemClock_Config(void);
static void MX_GPIO_Init(void);
static void MX_USART1_UART_Init(void);

int main(void) {
 HAL_Init();
 SystemClock_Config();
 MX_GPIO_Init();
 MX_USART1_UART_Init();
```

```
char rxData[50];

while (1) {
 HAL_UART_Receive(&huart1, (uint8_t*)rxData,
sizeof(rxData), HAL_MAX_DELAY);
 // Process received data (if needed)
 }
}

void SystemClock_Config(void) {
 // Configure the system clock as needed
}

static void MX_GPIO_Init(void) {
 // Initialize GPIO pins as needed
}

static void MX_USART1_UART_Init(void) {
 huart1.Instance = USART1;
 huart1.Init.BaudRate = 9600;
 huart1.Init.WordLength =
UART_WORDLENGTH_8B;
 huart1.Init.StopBits = UART_STOPBITS_1;
 huart1.Init.Parity = UART_PARITY_NONE;
 huart1.Init.Mode = UART_MODE_RX;
 huart1.Init.HwFlowCtl =
UART_HWCONTROL_NONE;
 HAL_UART_Init(&huart1);
```

}

In this example, STM32F446 is used as the transmitter and STM32F103 as the receiver. The transmitter sends data using UART to the HC-12 module, which wirelessly transmits the data to the HC-12 module connected to the receiver. The receiver receives the data through UART.

You'll need to connect the TX of STM32F446 to the RX of HC-12, and the TX of STM32F103 to the RX of the other HC-12 module. Make sure to configure the baud rate and other UART settings consistently on both sides.

Adjust the GPIO initialization, UART pins, and other settings according to your specific STM32 microcontroller and hardware configuration.

# INTERFACE 74HC4051 MULTIPLEXER WITH STM32 CUBEIDE HAL

I am using 74 HC 4051 multiplexer which can also be used as a D multiplexer This project will cover the multiplexing part I will cover D multiplexing. In near future I am connecting three potentiometers to three pins of the MUX and will read them using the single pin as input.

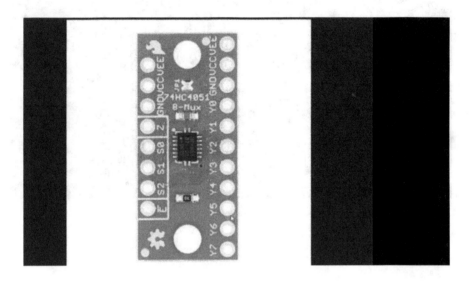

Let's start by creating a project and cube Id first I am using STM 32 F 446 R E but this should work across all STM devices give the name to the project and click Next just for confirmation the firmware version is one dot 24.1 First things first I am selecting the external crystal for the clock fours 051 mux have three select pins and one enable pin all these must be selected as output I am naming them to avoid confusion later let's take a look at the device itself. These are the select pins from s zero to s two enable pin is an active low pin.

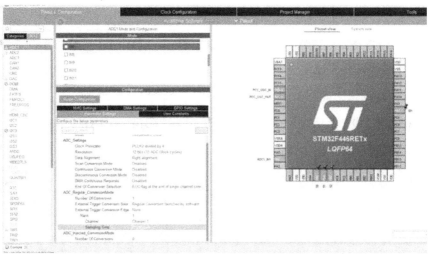

The select pins are used to control the I O pins from y zero to y seven and we have a Z pin which will connect to one of those IO pins. Let's see the datasheet of the device this is the block diagram of the device as you can see during the operation the Enable pin have to be low and which of the IO pins will connect to z can be controlled by using select pins as I mentioned I am going to read three potentiometers I am selecting ADC to do that the Z pin will be connected to PA one and I am leaving all the settings as it is except here I am increasing the sampling time setting up the clock for maximum frequency. Click Save to generate the code if we take a look at the main dot h file, we can see the names of the pins that we defined in the cube MX let's begin the coding process just defining a name to the port of select pins. This array will hold all the select pins the Select mux pin is used to select the respective i o pin of the multiplexer As mentioned in the datasheet we have to pull the Enable pin low for the MUX to work and to begin I am setting all the select pins to high now inside the while loop select the respective i o mux pin, start the ADC poll for conversion to complete before going further we need a variable to store these values.

So, I am defining a variable called value which can hold these eight values read the ADC value and finally stop the ADC this whole operation will continue for all the select PINs let's build this code and run it. I have only connected the sensors to first three pins of the MUX these all value seems to change randomly I will just use the first three pins of the MUX to display the result note that the values are now changing for only the first three variables note the changes happening in the value variable as I change the resistance in the potentiometer. This way we can read a different sensors using only one input pin and three select pins.

# EXAMPLE DUMMY CODE

Here's an example of how you can interface the 74HC4051 multiplexer with an STM32 microcontroller using the STM32CubeIDE and HAL (Hardware Abstraction Layer) libraries. The 74HC4051 is an 8-channel analog multiplexer/demultiplexer that can be controlled using digital signals.

In this example, I'll assume you want to use STM32's GPIO pins to control the multiplexer channels and read the analog signals using an ADC (Analog-to-Digital Converter) channel.

Create a New Project:

Open STM32CubeIDE and create a new project for your STM32 microcontroller.
Configure the Clock settings and other necessary configurations.
Configure GPIO and ADC:

Configure GPIO pins to control the selection lines (S0, S1, S2) of the 74HC4051.
Configure the ADC channel(s) to read the analog signals.
STM32CubeIDE Setup:

Enable the necessary GPIO and ADC peripherals in STM32CubeMX.
Configure the GPIO pins for output and the ADC channel(s) for analog input.
Example Code:
Here's a simplified example code to demonstrate the multiplexer interface and analog signal reading:

C

```
#include "main.h"
#include "stm32f4xx_hal.h"

ADC_HandleTypeDef hadc1;
uint16_t adcValue;

void SystemClock_Config(void);
static void MX_GPIO_Init(void);
static void MX_ADC1_Init(void);
```

```c
int main(void) {
 HAL_Init();
 SystemClock_Config();
 MX_GPIO_Init();
 MX_ADC1_Init();

 while (1) {
  for (int channel = 0; channel < 8; ++channel) {
   // Set multiplexer channel using GPIO pins
   HAL_GPIO_WritePin(GPIOB, GPIO_PIN_0,
(channel & 0x01));
   HAL_GPIO_WritePin(GPIOB, GPIO_PIN_1,
((channel >> 1) & 0x01));
   HAL_GPIO_WritePin(GPIOB, GPIO_PIN_2,
((channel >> 2) & 0x01));

   // Start ADC conversion
   HAL_ADC_Start(&hadc1);
   HAL_ADC_PollForConversion(&hadc1,
HAL_MAX_DELAY);
   adcValue = HAL_ADC_GetValue(&hadc1);

   // Process adcValue as needed
  }
 }
}

void SystemClock_Config(void) {
```

```c
// Configure the system clock as needed
}

static void MX_GPIO_Init(void) {
// Initialize GPIO pins as needed
__HAL_RCC_GPIOB_CLK_ENABLE();

GPIO_InitTypeDef GPIO_InitStruct = {0};
GPIO_InitStruct.Pin = GPIO_PIN_0 | GPIO_PIN_1
| GPIO_PIN_2;
GPIO_InitStruct.Mode =
GPIO_MODE_OUTPUT_PP;
GPIO_InitStruct.Pull = GPIO_NOPULL;
GPIO_InitStruct.Speed =
GPIO_SPEED_FREQ_LOW;
HAL_GPIO_Init(GPIOB, &GPIO_InitStruct);
}

static void MX_ADC1_Init(void) {
__HAL_RCC_ADC1_CLK_ENABLE();

ADC_ChannelConfTypeDef sConfig = {0};
hadc1.Instance = ADC1;
hadc1.Init.ClockPrescaler =
ADC_CLOCK_ASYNC_DIV1;
hadc1.Init.Resolution = ADC_RESOLUTION_12B;
hadc1.Init.ScanConvMode =
ADC_SCAN_DISABLE;
```

```
hadc1.Init.ContinuousConvMode = DISABLE;
hadc1.Init.DiscontinuousConvMode = DISABLE;
hadc1.Init.ExternalTrigConvEdge =
ADC_EXTERNALTRIGCONVEDGE_NONE;
hadc1.Init.ExternalTrigConv =
ADC_SOFTWARE_START;
hadc1.Init.DataAlign = ADC_DATAALIGN_RIGHT;
hadc1.Init.NbrOfConversion = 1;
HAL_ADC_Init(&hadc1);

sConfig.Channel = ADC_CHANNEL_0; // Adjust
ADC channel
sConfig.Rank = ADC_REGULAR_RANK_1;
sConfig.SamplingTime =
ADC_SAMPLETIME_3CYCLES;
HAL_ADC_ConfigChannel(&hadc1, &sConfig);
}
```

In this example, the GPIO pins control the multiplexer channels, and the ADC reads the analog signals from each channel. The STM32 reads the analog signal from each multiplexer channel sequentially.

Adjust the GPIO pins, ADC channel, and other settings according to your specific STM32 microcontroller and hardware configuration.

# BMP180 PRESSURE SENSOR WITH STM32 TEMPERATURE ALTITUDE CUBEIDE

I am using cube ID for the project. Let's take a look at the datasheet by the time Id gets ready here we have the measurement flow for the BMP 180. It's better explained in the later part of this document. This is the table for the oversampling setting, also known as Oss. Here you can control what type of calculation you want. I will be using O SS zero in my code, but you are free to choose other values too. Now this is the main algorithm for the measurement.

### 3.4 Calibration coefficients

The 176 bit E$^2$PROM is partitioned in 11 words of 16 bit each. These contain 11 calibration coefficients. Every sensor module has individual coefficients. Before the first calculation of temperature and pressure, the master reads out the E$^2$PROM data.
The data communication can be checked by checking that none of the words has the value 0 or 0xFFFF.

Table 5: Calibration coefficients

| Parameter | BMP180 reg adr | |
|---|---|---|
| | MSB | LSB |
| AC1 | 0xAA | 0xAB |
| AC2 | 0xAC | 0xAD |
| AC3 | 0xAE | 0xAF |
| AC4 | 0xB0 | 0xB1 |
| AC5 | 0xB2 | 0xB3 |
| AC6 | 0xB4 | 0xB5 |
| B1 | 0xB6 | 0xB7 |
| B2 | 0xB8 | 0xB9 |
| MB | 0xBA | 0xBB |
| MC | 0xBC | 0xBD |
| MD | 0xBE | 0xBF |

We will come back to this let's create the project in cube ID I am using STM 32 F four Discovery Board give some name to the project and click finish here is our cube MX let's clear the pin out first I am selecting external crystal for the main clock now as BMP 180 works with eye to see let's enable the eye to see one. In the later part of this project. I will also use the OLED display and for that I am selecting fast mode. You can use standard mode also. Let's see the clock setup now. I have eight megahertz crystal and the system is running at 168 megahertz click Save to generate the project here is our main file. Let's first include the library file for the BMP 180. Put the C file in the source and header file in the include directory. Include the BMP 180 dot h File in the Main. Let's see the BMP 180 dot h file. Here we have these functions available to be used in our main file. Start is to start the calibration to measure the temperature, pressure

141

altitude. Let's see how the code works. I have defined here the eye to see address for the BMP 180. So why the addresses zero cross double E.

Let's see the datasheet. Here we have the device address. We will assume that the LSB is zero then we have 111 here which corresponds to E in hexadecimal and we have 0111 in the higher nibble also. That's make the address zero cross double E Next, I have defined some variables here. Let's see the first half of them these 16 bit variables will be used to store the calibration data. And here are the approximate values for these variables. holes the rest of them are also mentioned in the datasheet. So, I have defined them too. VMP start calls a function read calibration data this function reads the calibration values from the E P rom of the BMP 180 As mentioned in the datasheet this zero cross double A is the start address for these registers.

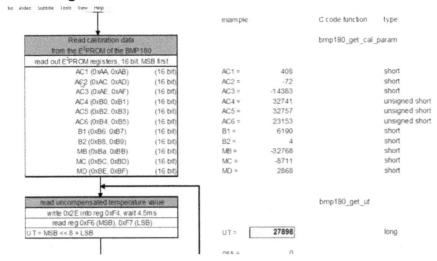

And starting from this address we need to read 22 registers totally I have used highlight to see memory read function to read the memory address. third parameter is the start address size of the start address and how many bytes to read a c one is a 16 bit variable and the registers are only eight bit in size we need to combine two registers to make them 16 bit in size and we need to do the same for all the calibration variables. Next part is to read the uncompensated temperature.

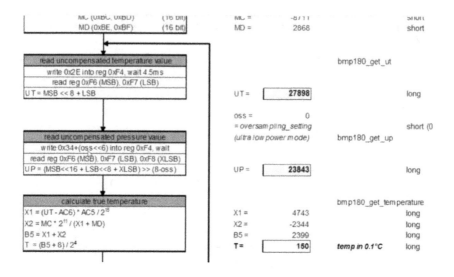

| MC (0x8C, 0x8D) | (16 bit) | MC = | -8711 | short |
| MD (0xBE, 0xBF) | (16 bit) | MD = | 2868 | short |

**read uncompensated temperature value** — bmp180_get_ut
write 0x2E into reg 0xF4, wait 4.5ms
read reg 0xF6 (MSB), 0xF7 (LSB)
UT = MSB << 8 + LSB

$UT = 27898$ — long

$oss = 0$
= oversampling_setting — short (0
(ultra low power mode)

**read uncompensated pressure value** — bmp180_get_up
write 0x34+(oss<<6) into reg 0xF4, wait
read reg 0xF6 (MSB), 0xF7 (LSB), 0xF8 (XLSB)
UP = (MSB<<16 + LSB<<8 + XLSB) >> (8-oss)

$UP = 23843$ — long

**calculate true temperature** — bmp180_get_temperature
$X1 = (UT - AC6) * AC5 / 2^{15}$ — $X1 = 4743$ — long
$X2 = MC * 2^{11} / (X1 + MD)$ — $X2 = -2344$ — long
$B5 = X1 + X2$ — $B5 = 2399$ — long
$T = (B5 + 8) / 2^4$ — $T = 150$ — *temp in 0.1°C* — long

To do that we need to write zero cross two e into the register zero cross F four and wait for 4.5 milliseconds so this is the data to write I am using memory write function this is the register and this here is the data and wait for five milliseconds Next we need to read starting from zero cross F six register and we need to read two bytes of the data as the manual says we need to read zero cross F six and F seven register for the MSB and lsb and finally convert them to a single 16 bit value to get the uncompensated temperature Next we need to read the uncompensated pressure but I preferred to do the calculation for the actual temperature these calculations here are as mentioned in the datasheet.

Now let's read the compensated pressure. To do so, we need to write zero cross three four along with the OSS in the register zero cross F four Hear O S S stands for over sampling setting it is explained in the table above. If you choose zero then the waiting period is 4.5 milliseconds. For any other selection waiting period also varies. This is the data to be written and we will write into into this register. I have covered different cases of OSS here. The code will wait according to your choice. Then we need to read the three registers starting from zero cross F six as mentioned in the datasheet we need to arrange these register values to get the uncompensated pressure This here is the calculation for actual pressure using the uncompensated value. This is exactly as mentioned in the manual we can calculate altitude from sea level using the pressure value. The formula to do so, is given here, here P is our actual pressure and P naught is the standard pressure at sea level standard pressure is defined as 101325 Pascal's This is how the library was written for the BMP 180. Now, let's start our program.

First of all, let's define the variables that we are going to store the values in. In the main function, start the BMP 180 to read the calibration data, these calibration values depends on the sensor. And that's why we need to calculate them once. Now in the while loop, we will calculate the temperature first, then pressure and then altitude. Let's wait for two seconds before repeating the calculations. Let's build our code. All good here, let Steve bucket I have added all the values in the expression on the right so that we can compare it with the values in the datasheet let's run it you can pause the project and compare these values. They are almost identical except a C one and a C two which have a huge difference. But that's okay and expected to as I mentioned earlier that the calibration values depends on the sensor and will vary for all you can see the temperature pressure and altitude values are precise and they are updating every two seconds. As I said during the setup that I will use OLED also, let's include the libraries for the display. OLED displays also connected to say my to see that his eye to see one copy see files in the source and the header files in the include. Let's include the header file first. These are the arrays where the characters corresponding to the float values will be stored let's initialize the OLED and print some strings on it. If you don't understand the OLED functions, check out the OLED project on the top right corner. Now after getting the values of temperature, pressure, and altitude, we will convert them to characters and display them on the OLED display. This is to display temperature, pressure and altitude. As you can see, we have some error here because we are trying to convert the float into the character. The solution is also provided by the ID so let's go to Project Properties. Build Settings tool setting and enable the blueprint float we also need to include the stdio dot h file for the S printf to work you can see the error is gone now. Let's build it and flashed to our board. You can see all the values are being displayed this is it for this project.

# EXAMPLE DUMMY CODE

Here's an example of how you can interface the BMP180 pressure and temperature sensor with an STM32 microcontroller using the STM32CubeIDE and HAL (Hardware Abstraction Layer) libraries. The BMP180 is a digital barometric pressure sensor that can be used to measure temperature, pressure, and calculate altitude.

Create a New Project:

Open STM32CubeIDE and create a new project for your STM32 microcontroller.
Configure the Clock settings and other necessary configurations.
Connect BMP180 Sensor:

Connect the SDA and SCL pins of the BMP180 to the appropriate GPIO pins on your STM32 microcontroller.
Connect the VCC and GND pins of the BMP180 to the appropriate power supply.
STM32CubeIDE Setup:

Enable the necessary I2C peripheral in STM32CubeMX.

Configure the I2C pins for communication with the BMP180 sensor.
Example Code:
Here's a simplified example code to demonstrate reading temperature and pressure values from the BMP180 sensor:

```c
#include "main.h"
#include "stm32f4xx_hal.h"
#include "bmp180.h"

I2C_HandleTypeDef hi2c1;

void SystemClock_Config(void);
static void MX_GPIO_Init(void);
static void MX_I2C1_Init(void);

int main(void) {
 HAL_Init();
 SystemClock_Config();
 MX_GPIO_Init();
 MX_I2C1_Init();

 BMP180_Init(&hi2c1);

 while (1) {
```

```
float temperature, pressure;

BMP180_GetTemperature(&temperature);
BMP180_GetPressure(&pressure);

// Calculate altitude based on pressure
float altitude =
BMP180_CalculateAltitude(pressure);

// Process temperature, pressure, and altitude
values as needed

HAL_Delay(1000); // Delay between
measurements
}
}

void SystemClock_Config(void) {
// Configure the system clock as needed
}

static void MX_GPIO_Init(void) {
// Initialize GPIO pins as needed
}

static void MX_I2C1_Init(void) {
hi2c1.Instance = I2C1;
hi2c1.Init.ClockSpeed = 400000; // I2C clock
```

```
speed
 hi2c1.Init.DutyCycle = I2C_DUTYCYCLE_2;
 hi2c1.Init.OwnAddress1 = 0;
 hi2c1.Init.AddressingMode =
I2C_ADDRESSINGMODE_7BIT;
 hi2c1.Init.DualAddressMode =
I2C_DUALADDRESS_DISABLE;
 hi2c1.Init.OwnAddress2 = 0;
 hi2c1.Init.GeneralCallMode =
I2C_GENERALCALL_DISABLE;
 hi2c1.Init.NoStretchMode =
I2C_NOSTRETCH_DISABLE;
 HAL_I2C_Init(&hi2c1);
}
```

In this example, the bmp180.h library
encapsulates the communication and calculations
required for the BMP180 sensor. Make sure you
have the necessary bmp180.h and bmp180.c files
in your project, containing functions to initialize,
read temperature, read pressure, and calculate
altitude using the BMP180 sensor.

Adjust the I2C pins, library functions, and other
settings according to your specific STM32
microcontroller and hardware configuration.

Remember to refer to the BMP180 datasheet,

# DWIN LCM WITH STM32 LED CONTROL USING BUTTONS

And today we will see how to interface this display with the STM 32 microcontroller. I would advise you guys to watch the Getting Started project first, as it will help you understand some concepts that I might skip in this project. The HMI displays mostly use you opted to communicate to the microcontrollers. So we are also going to use the UART to communicate with the STM 32. For this demonstration, I am going to control the LED on STM 32 Using the buttons on the D when LCD. Let's see the D win website again, go to downloads tools. We have already downloaded these files in the previous tutorial and today we will download the serial debugging assistant. This is needed to see the output of the LCD whenever we are performing some operations on it. We also need the development guide. So download this one. Everything you need to know is in this guide and I will explain the components I am going to use as the project progresses. Alright, let's start with the diga software create a new project and give it its location I have downloaded some bitmaps that I am going to use as the on off buttons. This is going to be the background image on the LCD. First of all we need to convert the images to proper size and generate the ICL files for the icons and images. So let's start with the picture conversion This is the image we want to resize select the screen resolution from here. Now click the image conversion and save it in the image folder inside the project. Now we will generate the ICL files for the background image and the icons select the background image that we just converted click on Generate ICL and we must save it in the D win set folder in our project. But what should we name this file? To understand it, we should look into the flash memory allocation. As mentioned here, the background picture I see URL addresses located at 32 We will also name it 32. Next we need to generate the ICL file for the icons we are using. Load the icons in the ICL generator and click Generate ICL.

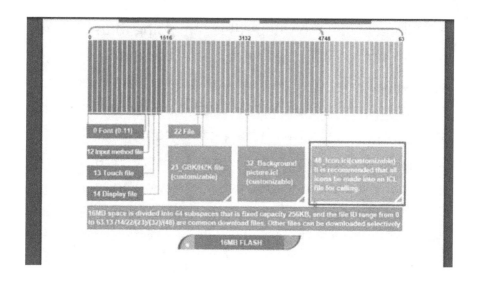

The ICL address for the icons is at 48. So we will name the file 48. This completes the ICL file generations for the assets we are using in this project. We also need to copy these icon files in the project folder. All right, now we can start designing the interface First, we will add the background image. Now to display the on off icons, we will use the variable icon control. You can find more about this variable icon in the development guide itself. As mentioned here, its function is to display different icons based on variable value. When the variable changes, the icons get switched to automatically. Here is the detail of the setting page for the variable icon. Anyway, I will explain these in detail while setting them up. Let's leave the SP to default. We are not covering that today. The V P stands for variable pointer and we will see it in the end. We need to set the icon file which is 48. In our case, the variable icon take Next the value from the variables stored at the variable pointer. Since we are using the on and off icons, we will keep the value of that variable as either zero or one, the minimum value of this variable is going to be zero, and we will set this green icon corresponding to this value. Similarly, the maximum value is going to be one, and we will set the red icon corresponding to this value. So basically when the variable is zero, it means the LED is off, and the LCD is going to display the green icon to turn on the LED. And when the variable is one, the LED will be on the LCD will display the red icon to turn off the LED. As I mentioned, the variable pointer is where the variable is going to store. This is basically a particular address in the RAM. And we can think of it as the address of some variable whose value we can change using some means. You can find more about the variable pointer in the development guide itself. If you notice here, the RAM is 128 kilobytes, which ranges from zero to FF FF with each address corresponding to two bytes. Out of this, the first eight kilobytes is reserved for the system variables, and the user can only access the addresses 1000 onwards. So I am going to set the variable pointer address to 1100 hexa. Now the variable icon will look for the value stored in this particular address. And based on that value, the icons will change automatically.

## 2.6 RAM Memory Variable Address Space

The RAM space is fixed at 128KB, which is divided into 0x0000-0xFFFF. Each variable address corresponds to 2 bytes of the corresponding space. A byte corresponds to 8 bits of the corresponding space.

Among them, 0x0000-0x0FFF is the system variable interface address space, which cannot be customized by the user; 0x1000-0xFFFF is available for users.

If 8-channel curves are used at the same time, 0x1000-0x4FFF will be used as the curve buffer address, at this time this part is occupied and cannot be used by other controls.

Then the user available address range is: 0x5000-0xFFFF.

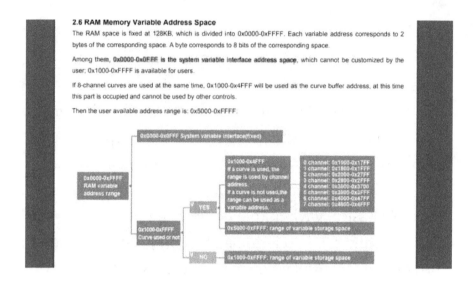

So we have set the variable pointer to look for the value stored of this particular address. But we also need to modify the value of this particular address. To do so we will use the incremental adjustment. This touch control will basically increment or decrement the value of the variable. You can find more details about it in the development guide. Check the data auto uploading, we will set the same variable pointer 1100 hexa. The adjust method is set to increment. So each time you touch the area, the value is going to increase. But we want the value to be either zero or one. So we'll set the overlimit to cycle. This will make sure that whenever the value has reached the maximum, the next touch will set the value to the minimum. The step length is one lower limit is zero, and the upper limit is one. So if the variable value is zero, the touch will incremented to one, and the next touch will reset it to zero and the process will continue. This way we will achieve what we want. The touch effect should be disposable so that long press will only register as a single click. All right, this is it for the configuration. Click Save and Generate the project. Before uploading the code to the LCD, you can debug it and check if everything is working. All right. The icons are changing whenever we tap on them. This means the variable is indeed incrementing and things are working fine. By the way, you can also modify the project and see the effect on the debugger window in real time. So this is very helpful if you are designing something big. Let's upload the code to the LCD. Select the D when SEC directory and it will automatically load the files needed to be flashed on the LCD. The LCD is connected to the comma 11 and the baud rate should be 11 Five 200 click stop downloading to download the project. Alright, everything is finished and you can see the LCD restarts with the new project we just copied the buttons are also responding well. So far everything is fine. Now we need to see what commands does this LCD send whenever we press these buttons. To know this, we will use the serial debugger we downloaded in the beginning to make sure the Comm port is set to a proper one and the baud rate is set to 11 Five 200.

Baud rate can be set, and the data frame consists of 5 parts.

| Data Block | 1 | 2 | 3 | 4 | 5 |
|---|---|---|---|---|---|
| Definition | Frame | Data length | Instruction | Data | CRC (optional) |
| Data Length | 2 | 1 | 1 | Max240 Bytes | |
| Description | 0x5AA5 | Instruction+data+CRC | 0x82Write 0x83Read | | |

The on/off of the CRC check is controlled by bit 0x05.7 of the .CFG file.

| Instruction Example | CRC Check Off | CRC Check On |
|---|---|---|
| 83 Read instruction | Tx:5A A5 04 83 000F 01 | Tx:5A A5 06 83 000F 01ED 90 |
| 83 Instruction reply | Rx:5A A5 06 83 00 0F 01 14 10 | Rx:5A A5 08 83 00 0F 01 14 10 43 F0 |
| 82 Write instruction | Tx:5A A5 05 82 10 00 31 32 | Tx:5A A5 07 82 10 00 31 32 CC 9B |
| 82 Instruction reply | Rx:5A A5 03 82 4F 4B | Rx:5A A5 05 82 4F 4B A5 EF |
| 83 Touch upload | Rx:5A A5 06 83 10 01 01 00 5A | Rx:5A A5 08 83 10 01 01 00 5A 0E 2C |

The LCD is displaying the green button. Let's press it you can see there is some commands sent by the LCD over the UART. Let's understand this command first Now we need to look into the data frame structure. Here you can see the first data block is the frame, which is basically the five a, a five in hexadecimal, we have also got exactly the same frame. The next block is the data length, which basically tells us how long the data is going to be. In our case, it's going to be six bytes long. These six bytes contain the instruction, the data itself and the CRC. The next block is the instruction. There are two instructions we can perform on the LCD. Zero cross 82 is to write something on the LCD and zero cross 83 is to read something from it. Here we are performing the read from the LCD. Basically, when we touch the area on the LCD, in a way, we are sending the read instruction to the LCD, and it replies back with the value of the variable pointer. After instruction, we have the data itself, which can be up to 249 bytes long. Let's see some examples to understand it better. This is the example to read the variable pointer. This here is the output from the LCD. First we have the frame data length and the read instruction. The next two bytes are the address of the variable pointer, which in our case is 1100. The same what we set in the incremental adjustment. After the address, there is one the number of words to read, we are also reading one word, the last two bytes are the values stored in the RAM address. In our case, the value is one. So we press the green button and the LCD sent one in the output and the button is red. Now on pressing the red button, everything is the same except the value is zero. Basically, when the LCD displays the green button, the LED will be off. On pressing the green button, the LCD will send one in the output which will turn on the LED the LCD will display the red button now and on pressing it the LCD will send a zero to the output which will turn off the LED. So all we have to look for is this last byte and whether this byte is one or zero will control the LED. If you count here, there are a total of nine bytes in this command. Let's keep that in mind. And now we will create a new project in STM 32. I am using the STM 32 F 103 controller and give some name to the project and click Finish. First of all we will do the clock setup. I am choosing the external high speed crystal for the clock. The blue pill has eight megahertz crystal and we will run the system at a maximum 72 megahertz frequency enable the serial wire debug. Now we will enable the UART to communicate with the LCD. I am choosing the UART one for this purpose. Make sure the baud rate is set to 11 Five 200 Leave everything to default here enable the interrupt as we are going to use interrupt to receive the data from the LCD. That's all the configuration required click Save to generate the project. By the way I have sold it a four pin header on the LCM module the module has the pins TX for TX two RX two and RX four I am connecting the TX two to the RX pin of the STM 32 and r x two to the TX pin of the STM 32 Let's write the code now. First of all we will define an array to store nine bytes of the data. Now in the main function, we will receive the UART data in the interrupt mode we will set the interrupt to trigger after nine bytes have been received. Once that happens, the receive complete callback will be called and we will write the rest inside it if you remember the while disables the interrupt after triggering it once. So we will again call the interrupt receive here. This will make sure the data is received continuously. Now the data is stored in the RX data array and if you remember only the last byte of this data is significant to us. We will process this data in the while loop. Here we will check the last byte of this array and if this byte is one we will turn on the LED at PC 13. The LED on the blue pill is active low, so to turn it on, we must pull the pin low. Similarly, if the last byte is zero, we will turn off the led by pulling it hi, I forgot to enable this PC 13 led in the cube MX set this pin to output and build the code again. All right, everything is set now build the code and debug it I am adding this RX data in the live expression. Since the LCD outputs the hexadecimal values we need to change the format to hexadecimal.

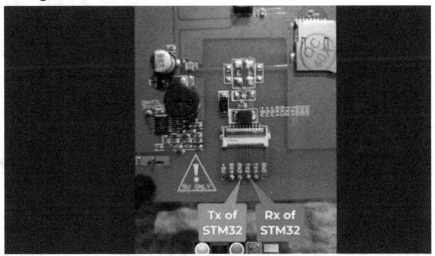

Remember that after changing it, you need to restart the debugger or else it won't show the correct values. Let's run the code now. Right now the green button is displaying on the LCD and the LED is turned off. When we press the button the LED turns on you can see the RX data array the last byte is one indicating to turn on the LED when the red button is pressed, the last byte is zero and the LED turns off you can see the LED is responding well with respect to the icons on the LCD. So I hope you understood how to interface this D when LCD with STM 32. You can interface it with any microcontroller which has the UART as it needs only you are to communicate.

# EXAMPLE DUMMY CODE

here's an example of how you can interface a 16x2 LCD (1602) with an STM32 microcontroller using parallel connection in 4-bit mode. This example uses the STM32CubeIDE and HAL (Hardware Abstraction Layer) libraries.

Create a New Project:

Open STM32CubeIDE and create a new project for your STM32 microcontroller.
Configure the Clock settings and other necessary configurations.
Connect LCD 1602:

Connect the RS, RW, E, and Data pins (D4-D7) of the LCD to the appropriate GPIO pins on your STM32 microcontroller.
Connect the VCC and GND pins of the LCD to the appropriate power supply.
STM32CubeIDE Setup:

Configure the GPIO pins for the LCD connections as output.
Initialize the necessary GPIO pins in the code.
Example Code:
Here's a simplified example code to demonstrate

displaying text on the LCD 1602 using 4-bit parallel connection:

C

```c
#include "main.h"
#include "stm32f4xx_hal.h"
#include <stdio.h>

#define LCD_RS_PIN GPIO_PIN_0
#define LCD_RS_PORT GPIOB
#define LCD_RW_PIN GPIO_PIN_1
#define LCD_RW_PORT GPIOB
#define LCD_E_PIN GPIO_PIN_2
#define LCD_E_PORT GPIOB
#define LCD_D4_PIN GPIO_PIN_3
#define LCD_D4_PORT GPIOB
#define LCD_D5_PIN GPIO_PIN_4
#define LCD_D5_PORT GPIOB
#define LCD_D6_PIN GPIO_PIN_5
#define LCD_D6_PORT GPIOB
#define LCD_D7_PIN GPIO_PIN_6
#define LCD_D7_PORT GPIOB

void SystemClock_Config(void);
static void MX_GPIO_Init(void);

void LCD_SendCommand(uint8_t cmd);
```

```c
void LCD_SendData(uint8_t data);
void LCD_Init(void);
void LCD_Clear(void);
void LCD_PrintString(char *str);

int main(void) {
 HAL_Init();
 SystemClock_Config();
 MX_GPIO_Init();

 LCD_Init();
 LCD_PrintString("Hello, STM32!");

 while (1) {

 }
}

void SystemClock_Config(void) {
 // Configure the system clock as needed
}

static void MX_GPIO_Init(void) {
 __HAL_RCC_GPIOB_CLK_ENABLE();

 GPIO_InitTypeDef GPIO_InitStruct = {0};
 GPIO_InitStruct.Mode =
GPIO_MODE_OUTPUT_PP;
```

```c
GPIO_InitStruct.Pull = GPIO_NOPULL;
GPIO_InitStruct.Speed = GPIO_SPEED_FREQ_LOW;

GPIO_InitStruct.Pin = LCD_RS_PIN | LCD_RW_PIN
| LCD_E_PIN |
    LCD_D4_PIN | LCD_D5_PIN | LCD_D6_PIN |
LCD_D7_PIN;

HAL_GPIO_Init(LCD_RS_PORT, &GPIO_InitStruct);
}

void LCD_SendCommand(uint8_t cmd) {
// Implement sending command to LCD using
GPIO pins
// For 4-bit mode, split data into nibbles and send
using D4-D7 pins
}

void LCD_SendData(uint8_t data) {
// Implement sending data to LCD using GPIO pins
// For 4-bit mode, split data into nibbles and send
using D4-D7 pins
}

void LCD_Init(void) {
// Implement LCD initialization sequence using
LCD_SendCommand
// Initialize LCD in 4-bit mode
```

```
}

void LCD_Clear(void) {
 LCD_SendCommand(0x01); // Clear display
command
 HAL_Delay(2); // Delay after clear command
}

void LCD_PrintString(char *str) {
 while (*str) {
 LCD_SendData(*str);
 str++;
 }
}
```

In this example, you need to implement the
LCD_SendCommand and LCD_SendData functions
to send the appropriate command and data to the
LCD using the GPIO pins. The LCD_Init function
initializes the LCD in 4-bit mode, and the
LCD_PrintString function sends a string to be
displayed on the LCD.

Adjust the GPIO pins, initialization sequence, and
other settings according to your specific STM32
microcontroller and hardware configuration.

Remember to refer to the LCD 1602 datasheet,

# LCD 1602 WITH STM32 PARALLEL CONNECTION 4 BIT MODE NOI2C

Without I to see this time in parallel connection LCD can work in two different modes, eight bit and four bit mode. In eight bit mode, we need to use all eight data pins and in four bit mode we can use only four data pins. We will use four bit mode in this tutorial.

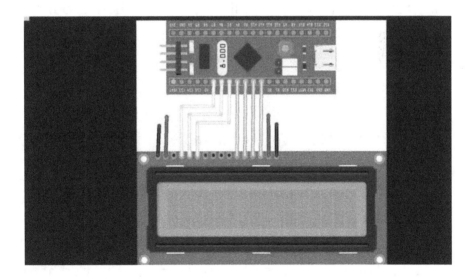

Let's start with the cube Id create a new STM 32 project I am using F 103 C eight controller give some name to the project and click Finish we have the cube MX here for the setup. I am enabling the external crystal for the clock enable the serial wire debug. We also need the delay in microseconds, so I am using timer one for the same. If you don't know about microsecond delay, check out the project on the top right corner. Let's set up the clock first. I want to run the controller of maximum possible frequency 72 megahertz. The APB two clock is also at 72 megahertz and timer one is connected to APB to a prescaler of 72 We'll divide the clock to one megahertz input the maximum possible value for the AR that is zero cross f f f as it is 16 bit register as shown in this picture pins pa one to PA seven are connected to the LCD we need to select them as output this is it for the setup. Now click Save and the project will be generated here is our main dot c file first of all we need to include the library files you can get these files after you download the project from the link in the description there is nothing special in the header file. These are the functions that you can use for the LCD. We need to modify things in the LCD 16 02 dot c file my connections is as shown in the picture from our s to enable pin and from D four to D seven you can use any pin and any port for the connection just make sure you define them properly here. Define the timer handler that you are using for the delay this function here is an internal function.

RS -> PA1
RW -> PA2
EN -> PA3
D4 -> PA4
D5 -> PA5
D6 -> PA6
D7 -> PA7

And it is not defined in the header file. sends to LCD is for writing the four bit data or command to the pins of the LCD. It takes two parameters. First is the useful data which is only four bits long and second is the R S. We update the pins to the rest Active bits in the data variable RS must be one for sending data and zero for sending command once the data is written to the pins, we will toggle the Enable pin. This will ensure that the data has been updated successfully. I am keeping this 20 microseconds delay commented out right now, we will see if it works without the delay or not. For higher clocks, this delay must be there. If the display shows some weird characters try increasing or reducing this delay. LCD send command is used to send the commands to the LCD. As we are only using four data pins are eight bit commands should also be divided into two four bit commands. That's why we need to send the command into two halves upper nibble, and lower nibble notes that are SS zero to indicate that it's a command LCD send data is used to send the data to the LCD. It uses the same process of sending the upper nibble first and then lower one the RS pin must be high to indicate that the data is being sent. LCD clear clears the LCD. Put cursor command is used to put the cursor at the entered location row can be zero or one and column can be from zero to 15. This function initializes the LCD in the four bit mode. These commands are written as per instructions in the datasheet then you have some display control functions here. You can modify them if you want some other configuration. For example if you want the blinking cursor use C and V as one in this command. Let's write the main code now. First, we need to include the header file make sure you stop the timer before initializing the LCD.

Now I am going to put the cursor at 00 and send some strings to the LCD and then put the cursor at first row and zero column and then send another string I want to wait for three seconds and then clear the display inside the while loop this function will print the ASCII characters from one to 128 build the code there are no errors let's flash it select STM 32 application click OK and wait for the debugger to launch as you can see the characters are being printed but quite not what we want. This is happening due to the delay missing in the Enable pin strobe. Let's enable the delay and flash the code again. If you face the problem again, try increasing or decreasing this delay. As you can see the data is being printed properly. Let me just reset the controller again. ASCII characters will continue to print from zero to 128 every 250 milliseconds.

# MOUSE AND KEYBOARD WITH STM32 USB HOST HID CUBEIDE HAL

I will show you how to interface a chai D with STM 32 I will interface both the mouse and the keyboard let's start by creating a project in cube Id first I am using STM 32 Discovery Board give some name to the project and click Finish let's clear the default pin outs first of all I am selecting the external crystal for the clock. Now go to USB OTG F s and enable the host only mode also enable the V bus so that we can provide power to the USB device go to USB host and enable the H I D class if you notice here, there is no solution found for the V bus. This is because we haven't enabled the power supply yet. Open the user manual for your board as you can see here the supply for the V bus can be enabled by the pin PCs zero it is connected to enable pin which is active low pin so to turn on the power supply we need to pull the pin PCs zero to low and then this three volts supply will be activated for the V bus pin select the pin PCs zero as output as you can see now there is a solution for the V bus.

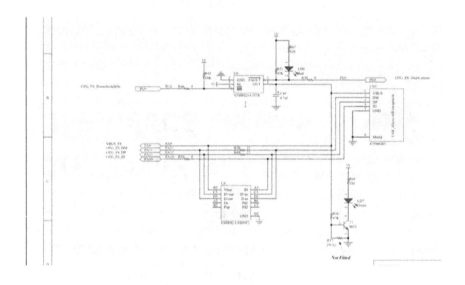

Let's enable the UART so that we can see the output on the console now the clock setup I have eight megahertz external Crystal and I want the system to run at maximum clock this is it for the setup click Save to generate the project here is our main file first of all let's include the USB h h ID dot c file we will be using the functions from this file here we are interested in H ID event callback function. This will be called whenever we receive any data event. This is a common function for both the mouse and the keyboard. So we need to check if the data is received from the mouse or from the keyboard. A Chai D get device type will be used for this purpose if the data is received from the mouse, we will perform the operations here. And we will write a similar function for the keyboard first define a pointer to the mouse info type def. Basically, this structure will contains all the data from the mouse that we will receive The data contains the movement in x axis in Y axis and the indication of which button is pressed on the mouse here we will receive and store the data in the structure the movement in the x and the y axis ranges from zero to 255 and that's why it is hard to understand the movement to make it look simpler I am making some modifications here this way the movement in one direction will be positive while in the other direction it will be negative now we will store all these values in a buffer and finally send them to you art we will do the same steps for the keyboard also first define the keyboard type def then get the keyboard data and store it into the structure in keyboard we have a function to get the ASCII code of the key that was pressed we will get the ASCII code from the structure where we stored the data and store it in a variable now store all these values in a buffer and finally send them to you art let's build this code now some error in the variables here let me just quickly fix that also let's add the STD I O dot h for the S printf to work now everything is good. Let's flash this to the board. I am connecting the mouse via the OTG cable, open the serial monitor to view the data Move the mouse to the left.

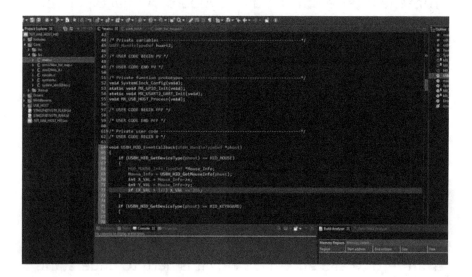

As you can see the x values are negative you can observe how the values are changing. They decreased from zero to minus four minus 12 minus 20 to minus 30. Basically the faster you move, the higher this value will be. And as the mouse slows down, the values started increasing and finally becomes zero when the mouse stops. This is the movement in the right direction. The x values are positive now they follow the same pattern as they did in the left direction. Now as I am moving the mouse up, the y value is changing in the negative direction. The mouse is moving down this time. Y values are positive and almost no change in x values. Now let's test the buttons. This is the left click, you can see the button one value was one when I pressed the button and becomes zero when I release it. For the right click button two value becomes one when I pressed the button and becomes zero when I release it, and for the middle click the button three value changes. Let's see one more time. Left click, right click, middle click. This is it for the mouse. Now let's remove the mouse and connect the keyboard. We will keep our program running as we have included both the mouse and keyboard in our callback function. So when we press the key, the character get displayed. And when we release the key and all gets displayed. We can print the capital characters, numbers, symbols etc. During testing, I found that the Bluetooth mouse and keyboards don't work properly, so try using the wired ones. I hope you guys understood this project. I will try to make use of this in my upcoming projects where I will try to display the movement of the mouse and the keyboard characters on the TFT display.

# EXAMPLE DUMMY CODE

Here's an example of how you can interface a USB mouse and keyboard with an STM32 microcontroller using USB Host HID (Human Interface Device) communication via the STM32CubeIDE and HAL (Hardware Abstraction Layer) libraries.

This example will cover detecting and interacting with a USB mouse and keyboard.

Create a New Project:

Open STM32CubeIDE and create a new project for your STM32 microcontroller.
Configure the Clock settings and other necessary configurations.
USB Host Setup:

Enable USB Host and HID support in STM32CubeMX.
Configure the USB pins for communication with the USB devices.
STM32CubeIDE Setup:

Configure USB Host class and HID class in STM32CubeMX.

Enable the necessary GPIOs and USB peripherals in STM32CubeMX.
Example Code:
Here's a simplified example code to demonstrate detecting and interacting with USB mouse and keyboard:

```c
#include "main.h"
#include "usb_host.h"
#include "usbh_hid.h"

USBH_HandleTypeDef hUSB_Host;

void SystemClock_Config(void);

int main(void) {
 HAL_Init();
 SystemClock_Config();

 USBH_Init(&hUSB_Host, USBH_UserProcess, 0);
 USBH_RegisterClass(&hUSB_Host,
USBH_HID_CLASS);

 while (1) {
  USBH_Process(&hUSB_Host);
 }
}
```

```c
void SystemClock_Config(void) {
 // Configure the system clock as needed
}

void USBH_UserProcess(USBH_HandleTypeDef
*phost, uint8_t id) {
 switch (id) {
  case HOST_USER_SELECT_CONFIGURATION:
   break;
  case HOST_USER_DISCONNECTION:
   // Handle disconnection event
   break;
  case HOST_USER_CLASS_ACTIVE:
   // Device (mouse or keyboard) detected and
ready
   break;
  case HOST_USER_CONNECTION:
   // Handle USB device connection
   break;
  default:
   break;
 }
}

void
USBH_HID_EventCallback(USBH_HandleTypeDef
*phost) {
```

```
// Handle HID events (mouse or keyboard data)
}
```

In this example, the USBH_UserProcess function handles various events like USB device connection, disconnection, and configuration selection. The USBH_HID_EventCallback function is a callback that can be used to handle HID events and data received from the connected USB HID device (mouse or keyboard).

Make sure you've enabled the appropriate USB pins, configured USB Host and HID classes, and implemented the necessary callback functions and data processing logic.

Remember to refer to the STM32 reference manual, USB Host library documentation, and specific STM32CubeIDE documentation for accurate details and implementation guidelines.

# ST7920 GLCD WITH STM32 SERIAL MODE F103 CUBEMX

I am using STM 32 F 103 controller and I will explain you all the functions using datasheet so watch the entire project properly let's start by creating the project in cube MX first in this tutorial I will use the serial connection for the SP 7920 And for that we have to select four pins as output from the controller. I will explain about these pins in a while Next, we have to use some delays in microseconds and so I am going to select a timer to create those delays. I have already made a project about this topic you can watch on the top right corner of your device also I will leave the link in the description now complete the rest of the setup and open the project next we need to copy the delay library and the SG 7920 library files into the project and after copying them also include them in the project. Let's take a look at the delay library. As I am using time one for the delay I am going to make some changes here in the timer handler that sit for the timer set up in the library. Let's build this and check for the errors if any. Everything looks good till now. Let's take a look at the st 7920 library file and see how these functions work. So about those four pins we selected his output in the cube MX they are connected as follows. A five is connected to enable in the LCD. A six is connected to RS pin of the LCD. A seven is connected to RW pin of the LCD.

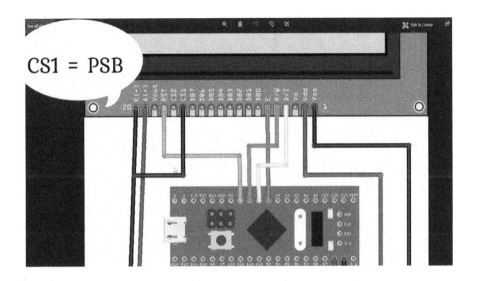

B zero is connected to reset pin of the LCD. This is the connection of the microcontroller to the LCD. This is a five pin this is a six pin this is a seven pin this is B zero pin and this one here is P SP which should be grounded to use the serial mode if you are using any other pinout you must define here about the clock see s s ID and reset pins. Up So first of all this function replaces the SPI transfer SPI doesn't always works for me so I intend not to use it. Here also we can transfer the data same way as the SPI does and that is first strike the bid either high or low, and then toggle the clock next sending commands to the LCD. Now, if you take a look at the data sheet, it says that when CS will be high only then the clock will be accepted.

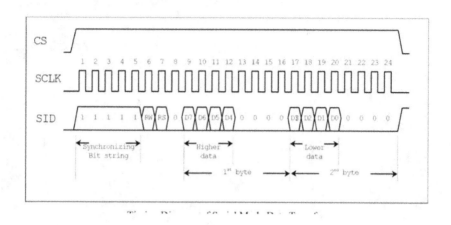

So first we will pull the cspn pi next before sending the actual command or data we have to send a synchronizing byte which consists of zero cross F eight and then our W RS and zero for sending the command we have to make Rs zero after sending the synchronizing byte we have to send higher data byte followed by lower byte. And at last pull the CS back to low indicating end of transfer data is also sent in the same way except this time RS will be one in the synchronizing byte. Next, in order to initialize the LCD, we have to follow some pattern of commands. First of all, we have to toggle the reset and wait for more than 40 milliseconds. Next, we have to send the function set command for the eight bit mode and wait for more than 100 microseconds. Again send the function set command for the eight bit mode and wait for more than 37 microseconds. Next, send the display on off control command and wait for more than 100 microseconds. I am keeping everything zero right now. We will turn it on in the end. Next send the display clear command and wait for more than 10 milliseconds and in the end, send the entry mode command to increment cursor to the right with no shift and turn that is play on this ends the initialization of the LCD. To turn on the graphic display again we have to follow some set of commands.

- **FUNCTION SET**

RS RW DB7 DB6 DB5 DB4 DB3 DB2 DB1 DB0

| 0 | 0 | 0 | 0 | 1 | DL | X | RE | x | x |

Code

**DL : 4/8 BIT interface control bit**

When DL = "1",  **8 BIT** MPU bus interface

When DL = "0",  為 **4 BIT** MPU bus interface

**RE : extended instruction set control bit**

When RE = "1", extended instruction set

When RE = "0", basic instruction set

**In same instruction cannot alter DL and RE at once. Make sure that change DL first then RE.**

- **SET CGRAM ADDRESS**

RS RW DB7 DB6 DB5 DB4 DB3 DB2 DB1 DB0

| 0 | 0 | 0 | 1 | AC5 | AC4 | AC3 | AC2 | AC1 | AC0 |

First select the eight bit mode then turn on the extended instruction set and at last the graphic mode we have to write them separately as mentioned in the datasheet. To draw any graphic to the display, we have to first set the vertical coordinates and then the horizontal coordinates of the display after that write the upper byte followed by the lower byte and we do the same for the bottom half of the screen also, display clear command can clear display in both graphic mode and text mode. Since string command can print the string on the specific row and column of the display, this only works in the text mode let's write the program and display something now. First, we have to initialize the delay and then initialize the LCD. Here I am writing few strings to different rows and columns of the display let's build it and flash it to the microcontroller. Of course there is our usual error about the resetting go to the configuration debugger, generate a script and change it to software system reset so as you can see, it works pretty well let's try to display a bitmap on this display now. I have this image here of the s t and I will use GIMP to convert it to the BMP format go to the Image Mode index and change it to the one bit black and white. Okay, things don't look good here. This is probably due to the saturation of colors. Let's fix it follow closely what I am doing.

And now, if you change it you will get the black and white image next change the size and export it to the BMP format. Next I am using LCD assistant for changing it to the hex format Copy the code inside the program I already have a bitmap dot h file and I am going to copy in this itself right now I have two bitmaps and I will display them both we have to first turn on the graphic mode I am going to display a bitmap than wait for few seconds then after clearing it display the another bitmap I forgot to include the header file in the project Okay, let's build it and display on the LCD as you can see this is the first bitmap and this is the second one I will reset the controller one small other than these we can also draw different shapes such as circles, triangles, rectangles, and so on.

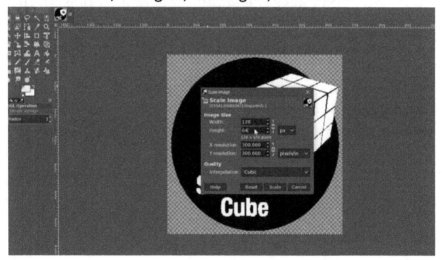

I have just put them at random places. Here you can see all of these functions together. Remember that if you want to write the text again, you have to disable the graphic mode.

# STONE HMI DISPLAY WITH STM32 LED CONTROL PRINT VALUES ON THE DISPLAY

I have already explained how the display communicates using the UART in the previous project and today we will continue where we left last time. Here is the picture of the display. Here you can see that Assam pins available to connect directly with the controller but the spacing is too wide and I don't have the appropriate header pins for this. So I am going to use the UART to USB board that comes along with the display as it has some set of pins which can be used as the TX and RX pins. After doing some continuity testing, I have found out that the TX B is connected to this particular pin right here and the RX B is connected to this particular pin.

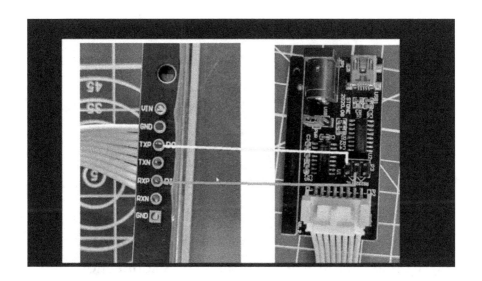

We have already discussed that the stone HDMI outputs the data in the RS 232 format. So in order to convert it to the TTL I'm using this Rs 232 to TTL converter. This is the pin out for the TTL converter. And as you can see on the top row the middle pin which is pin number three is the RX pin and pin number two is the TX pin.

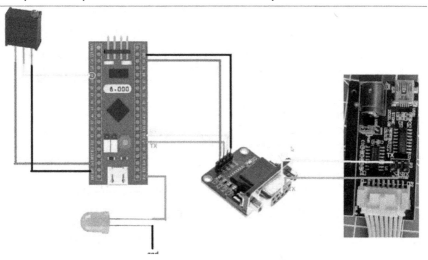

There are other pins but we are only interested in these two. Here is the connection diagram. The TX pin from the board connects with the RX pin of the converter and the RX pin from the board connects the TX pin this converter is powered by five volts which is provided by the STM 32 itself. I tried using the 3.3 volts but it was not working properly. Anyway the TX pin from the converter connects with the TX pin of the STM 32 and the RX pin connects with the RX pin. One very important thing you have to notice that on this side we have a cross connection between TX and RX pins but on the controller side there should be a straight connection TX connecting with the TX and RX connecting with RX. We also have a potentiometer which is connected to the pin PA zero that's going to be the ADC pin and is powered by the 3.3 volts we have an LED which is going to be controlled by the buttons on the display. This led is connected to pin PV 12. All right let's see the design now. I am going to continue from the previous design. This is the label we had in the previous project along with the two more labels that I added for this project. This particular label is going to act as the indicator of the LED state so whenever we press the button it's going to show the current state of the LED let's rename this to led off by default and later we will change this within the code itself. This label to is going to display this string and it will remain unchanged. We have one more label which is label three that's where the value of the potentiometer is going to display so there are not

188

many changes I have made here. Let's just save this project and we will copy this into the display itself Alright, let's create a new project in STM 32. I am using the STM 32 F 103 ch controller give some name to the project and click Finish I am using the external crystal for the clock also configure the serial wire debug and change the time base to sis tick. Let's configure the clock now. As usual we will use the external eight megahertz crystal and the system will be running at 72 megahertz. Now we will configure the UART I am using the UART one and you can see the pins pa nine and Pa 10 have been selected as the TX and RX pins. We will keep the settings as default just enable the interrupt. Let's set the pin PB 12 as the output pin for the LED. We also need to configure the ADC Channel Zero so that pin PA zero is selected As the ADC pin, not much of the configuration is required for the ADC, and since we will be using the poll method, even if you keep everything default, it will be fine. Click Save to generate the project. I think there is some problem with the clock. Let's check it out. Just click Yes to resolve the issue. All right now click Save to generate the project. First of all, we need to check if we are receiving the data. So I'm calling the whole UART receive in the blocking mode, and I am receiving the 50 bytes of the data or two seconds of the timeout, whichever triggers first, let's define the RX data here. Now build the code and D pocket I have added the RX data in the live expression. So we have hit the breakpoint. And if you see the RX data, we have received 36 bytes in total. As we have already discussed in the previous project, when we press the button, the display sends one set of data. And when we release the button, it sends another set. So these 36 Bytes actually contain the two sets of data with 18 bytes each. If you notice here, we do have the button name led 01, which we set in the Designer software. Now let's check the instruction manual. Here you can see on pressing the button, it sends the seven bytes of data followed by the button name and its state, these seven bytes of data remain constant for whatever button you're pressing, and the button name is going to change as per what we have defined in the Designer software, then the last five bytes will be the terminating ones. So we have the first seven fixed bytes, plus the last five fixed bytes plus five bytes of our button name and one byte for the state. Totally the 18 bytes of the data. And this is the reason why I mentioned that if we keep the button names of the same length, it will be better for us to program it since we are going to receive the same amount of data on pressing both the buttons. So even if you want to program it in a simple way, by using just the blocking functions, receiving the fixed amount of data, it can work pretty well. But I am not going to do that. And that's why I am using the receive to idle function in interrupt mode. If you have been following my projects, you would know about this function, since we have already covered it in one of the UART projects. Basically, this function triggers the interrupt whenever it detects the idle line, which is when the controller is not receiving the data for some fixed amount of time. This interrupt will call the interrupt handler where we will write the rest of the code for now I am just calling the same function again because we know hold disables the interrupt after one call. So we need to call it again. All right, let's write the rest of the code now, I am defining the pointer to the TX data that we will send to the display these received variable will be set whenever we receive some data from the display. And if this variable is set, we will proceed with the rest of the code inside the while loop. Here we will first check the received data and we will look for the button name. Note here that we are checking the received data from the seventh position. This is because of the data pattern. As mentioned in the instruction manual. The first seven bytes are always the constants and the button names starts from the seventh position. So in our case, we will get L Ed 01. And we are basically comparing that particular string with the received data. Once the string matches the string compare functions are put his going to be zero and that will indicate the on button has been pressed. Since the on button is pressed, we will turn on the LED by setting the pin Hi.

| | | | set a custom key value, the system key value is delivered by default, if the user key value is set, the user-defined key value is delivered |
|---|---|---|---|
| LEN | "widget name" + length of user key value | data length | |
| DATA | widget name + user key value | data content | The last two bytes of the data part; high-order first, low-order last |

2. For example:
   System key value:
a) Button press instruction:
   Response: ST<0x10 0x01 0x00 0x08 button9 0x01>ET
   HEX:53 54 3C 10 01 00 08 62 75 74 74 6F 6E 39 01 3E 45 54 E7 E0

b) Click button and release (complete button click action) instruction:
   Response: ST<0x10 0x01 0x00 0x08 button9 0x02>ET
   HEX:53 54 3C 10 01 00 08 62 75 74 74 6F 6E 39 02 3E 45 54 A3 E0

Then we will reset the receipt variable so that we don't enter this loop again. Now we have to send the state of the LED to label one. To do so we will first allocate the memory for the TX data. I am allocating 100 bytes for it. Then copy this entire string into the TX data To understand this string let's go back to the instruction manual. And here we will see the label section. As mentioned here, this is the command we need to send in order to display some string on the HMI module. So I am using the S printf function to copy that entire command into the TX data buffer. This entire command needs to be in the string format so we need to put it inside double quotes also note that the command itself contains a lot of double quotes. To handle this we need to put the backward slash before every double quote inside the command the text we are sending is led on also the label is label one. Basically the type is label and which it name

192

is label one. Once the data is copied into the TX data, we will send it using the transmit function. And finally we will free the memory allocated for the TX data. Similarly, if the received data contains LEDs 02 that means the off button must have been pressed, we will perform the same things just this time the LED will be turned off and the text will be led off. All right, let's build and debug this code. We have few warnings. And that might be because I didn't include a few of the header files. So let me do that quickly. All right, all the errors are gone now, and we can debug the code. You can see the LED is turned on. Here is the RX data. Notice that this time we have only received 18 bytes of data. Well, this is because there is a small delay between when we press the button and release it. So the received to idle function triggers twice when we pressed the button. And when we released it. When this function triggers second time, it overwrites the data from the first part. This is not a problem for us, since we are only looking for the button name. And as long as that particular button is being pressed or released, the code will still work. Keep a note of this particular value here as this is the only difference between the two buttons. So you can see the LED is responding according to the buttons we are pressing. Also notice that the LED state is changing as well. So this part is working well so far, and we can proceed ahead now we need to implement the ADC and display the potentiometer value on the third label we created in the Designer Software. As I mentioned in the beginning, I am going to use the poll method for the ADC. So here we just need to start the ADC, then pull for the conversion, then get the ADC value and finally stop the ADC.

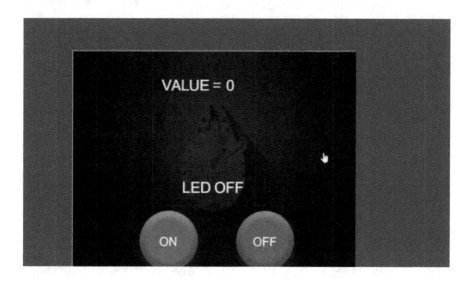

Now we need to send this value to the module, we will use the same method that we have used so far. allocate the memory for the TX data buffer and then copy the command into this TX data. But here instead of the text, we will pass the format specifier in the s printf function percent U is used as a format specifier for the unsigned values and we are using the unsigned 16 bit variable. The label is labeled three as we have already defined in a Designer Software. After the data has been copied into the TX data buffer, we will simply send it to the UART and clear the memory located for the TX data. I am giving 100 milliseconds delay in the while loop so that the ADC can get some time before the next run. All right now let's build the code In D bucket you can see the value of the potentiometer is being displayed on the top label. As I am rotating the potentiometer the value is also changing the buttons are working as usual and the LED state is also indicating correctly, everything is working as expected. So today we saw how we can receive the data from the HMI module and display some data on it, we were able to display the string and the value of the potentiometer itself.

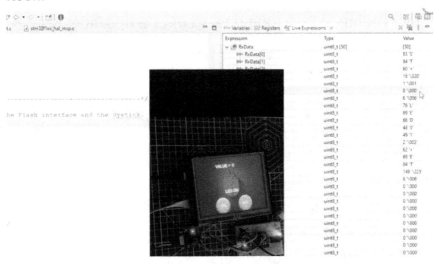

I hope you understood the project. The purpose of using the receive to idle function was that even if your project doesn't have all the elements with the same name, or don't send the same amount of data, the receive to idle function can handle it and it will only trigger the interrupt once the entire data has been transferred. You can still use the regular UART functions. If you are sure about the length of the data you are going to receive.

# TFT DISPLAY WITH STM32 IN PARALLEL MODE CUBEIDE CUBEMX HAL

This is going to be a long ride, so buckle up kindly pay attention to every detail there are a lot of settings involved. I am using HDX 347 G display and it is 240 by 320 TFT display as shown in the picture. Before starting this tutorial, I want to mention that this is a port from MCU friends is Arduino code I have made some changes to make it compatible with cube MX let's start by creating the project in cube ID I am using STM 32 F 103 controller the method should work with others too. I have tested it on f 446 and F 407 controllers.

Okay, first things first set up the RCC and serial wire debug we need the delay in microseconds. So I am using timer one to do that I am assuming I don't need to explain this part. You can check my other project if you don't know how to use delay in microseconds. Here comes the main part. All these TFTs have eight data pins and five control pins. It will be good for you if you choose the port pins of any one port from zero to seven to connect them in the same order to the LCD data pins. But just to show you guys how to program in the random cases, I will choose some of the pins as random. Here I am choosing PB zero and PB one and then 3456 to be connected in the same order to the LCD data pins than p a five to be connected to LCD D seven and p a 15 to LCG de to pin the connections are as follows D zero d one d two d three D four D five d six D seven we have to select five control pins also. This is for reset than CS than WR than R S and finally our D is selected as input the final setup of the pins is as shown in the picture. Next complete the rest of the setup for the clock and once done just click save. Now we need to copy some library files into the project folder just follow me. Let's just refresh the project once. Next, we need to include those files in our project If you take a look at the functions dot h file, these are all the functions that you can use for the TF t all the modification that you are required to do is in the User Settings dot h file I forgot to include the functions dot h file coming back to modification first of all change the pins and ports according to your setup most of them are fine let's take a look at the connections once LCD D seven is connected to GPIO A five I need to change that hear you define the width and height of the LCD hear you need to uncomment the type of display you are using.

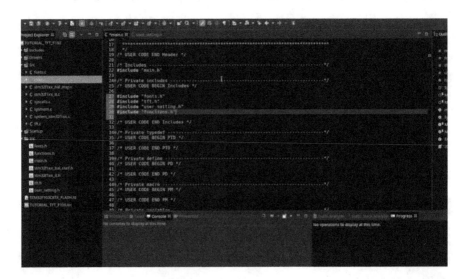

I am using h x 8347 G so that one is defined microsecond delay function is defined here, change it accordingly. If you are not using timer one, here comes the most important part of the setup. I have even written everything in the comments, you can read it. Here, we are going to modify the Rite Aid function. First, we need to clear all the data pins. And to do that, we need to set the higher bits of BSR register. For example, to clear pins B three before B eight and benign we will write one to third, fourth, eighth and ninth position and shifted left 16 times. So in the GPI OB BSSR register, I am going to write one in zeroeth first, third, fourth, fifth and sixth positions because these are the GPI OB pins that are connected to LCD data pins. For GPIO, a only pins a two and a 15 are connected to the LCD data pins.

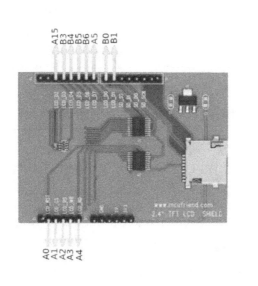

So one is only written in the fifth and 15th position. Next, we need to write data to these pins. And to do so we will write to the lower bits of BSS or register. Here, I have mentioned an example that if LCD D four is connected to B seven, and LCD D six is connected to b two. Then in order to write the data, we need to select the fourth bit of data because we are doing it for LCD D four and then shift that bit by three to make it seven. That's where the D four is connected. And similarly, to write to the LCD D six, we will first select the sixth bit of data and this time, we will shift it to the right by four. That will be like subtracting and the final result would be two. That's where the D six is connected. In our actual case, the LCD D two pin is connected to a 15 so In the GPIO A BSS or register we need to first select the second bit and then shifted by 13 to make a total of 15 also LCD D seven is connected to a five so first we will select the seventh bit of the data and then we need to shift that bit to fifth location so shifted right by two Next, coming to GPIOB LCD D zeros connected to the zero pin, so we don't need to shift it anywhere. Similarly, other pins are also connected in a proper order. So no shifting is required. That's why I told you to choose and connect in order it makes things are a bit easy. This was the writing data to the pins. Now to read the value on the pins, we need to read the input data register. Again, I have mentioned an example here you can read it basically Unlike last time, where we selected the

LCD pins first here we are going to select the GPIO pins first.

```
// configure macros for the data pins.
/* First of all clear all the LCD DATA pins i.e. LCD_D0 to LCD_D7
 * We do that by writing the HIGHER bits in BSRR Register
 *
 * For example :- To clear Pins B3, B4 , B8, B9, we have to write GPIOB->BSRR = 0x0000001100011000 <<16
 *
 *
 * To write the data to the respective Pins, we have to write the lower bits of BSRR :-
 *
 * For example say the PIN LCD_D4 is connected to PB7, and LCD_D6 is connected to PB2
 *
 * GPIOB->BSRR = (data & (1<<4)) << 3.  Here first shift the data bit by 4 (LCD_D4), and than again shift left by 3 (Total 4+3 =7
 *
 * GPIOB->BSRR = (data & (1<<6)) >> 4.  Here first shift the data bit by 6 (LCD_D6), and than again shift Right by 4 (Total 6-4 =
 */
#define write_8(d) { \
 GPIOA->BSRR = 0b1000000000100000 << 16; \
 GPIOB->BSRR = 0b0000000001111011 << 16; \
 GPIOA->BSRR = (((d) & (1<<2)) << 13); \
 GPIOB->BSRR = (((d) & (1<<0)) << 8) \
             | (((d) & (1<<1)) << 0) \
             | (((d) & (1<<3)) << 0) \
             | (((d) & (1<<4)) << 0) \
             | (((d) & (1<<5)) << 0) \
             | (((d) & (1<<6)) << 0) \
             | (((d) & (1<<7)) << 0); \
 }

/* To read the data from the Pins, we have to read the IDR Register
 *
 * Take the same example say LCD_D4 is connected to PB7, and LCD_D6 is connected to PB2
 *
 */
```

After selecting the GPIO pin, we will shift it to make it equal to the LCD pin it is connected to you will get an idea of what I am talking about in a while. Let's take the zero first it is connected to D zero so we won't shift it same for the B one also. Now here I have selected a 15 and as it is connected to LCD D two is shifting it by 13 to the right 15 minus 13 makes up two next B three B four B five and the six are connected to the respective pins so no shifting is required. Now in the end, I am selecting pin a five and then shifting it by two in the left to make it seven because a five is connected to LCD D seven. This completes the important part of the setup next you need to uncomment these lines based on your clock frequency. Let's write the main function now. I am defining a variable to store ID of the LCD Next, we need to stop the timer for the delay to work first of all, read the ID of the display and store it in the variable that we created. Give some delay.

```
104
105    ID = readID();
106
107    HAL_Delay(100);
108
180    tft_init (ID);
110
111    setRotation(0);
112
113    fillScreen(BLACK);
114
115    testFillScreen();
116    testLines(CYAN);
117    testFastLines(RED, BLUE);
118    testFilledCircles(10, MAGENTA);
119    testCircles(10, WHITE);
120
121    fillScreen(BLACK);
122
123    /* USER CODE END 2 */
124
125    /* Infinite loop */
126    /* USER CODE BEGIN WHILE */
127    while (1)
128    {
129      /* USER CODE END WHILE */
130
131      /* USER CODE BEGIN 3 */
132    }
133    /* USER CODE END 3 */
134 }
```

Next, initialize the TFT with the ID than I am writing some tests okay prints new STR prints the string in a row its parameters are the row number text color the font type that you can find in the fonts dot c file size of the text and the string itself and in the end I am putting the display in the continuous scrolling let's compile the code and debug it I am setting the live expression to monitor the ID so, I am getting correct ID here I will continue the execution you can see all the tests being performed by the display let's put this outside the while loop and I will add a code to invert the display correct the size of the string also let's disable these and run the program again. So, the things are working as expected.

# EXAMPLE DUMMY CODE

Here's an example of how you can interface a TFT display with an STM32 microcontroller using parallel mode. This example uses the STM32CubeIDE and HAL (Hardware Abstraction Layer) libraries.

Please note that interfacing a TFT display in parallel mode requires a significant amount of code, and the exact implementation might vary based on the specific TFT display model you are using. This example provides a basic framework that you can adapt to your specific TFT display's requirements.

Create a New Project:

Open STM32CubeIDE and create a new project for your STM32 microcontroller.
Configure the Clock settings and other necessary configurations.
Connect TFT Display:

Connect the data lines (D0-D7) and control lines (RS, WR, RD, CS, RST) of the TFT display to the appropriate GPIO pins on your STM32 microcontroller.

Connect the VCC and GND pins of the TFT display to the appropriate power supply.
STM32CubeIDE Setup:

Configure the GPIO pins for the TFT display connections as output.
Initialize the necessary GPIO pins in the code.
Example Code:
Here's a simplified example code to demonstrate initializing and clearing the TFT display:

C

```c
#include "main.h"
#include "stm32f4xx_hal.h"

#define TFT_RS_PIN GPIO_PIN_0
#define TFT_RS_PORT GPIOB
// Define other TFT control pins and data pins

void SystemClock_Config(void);
static void MX_GPIO_Init(void);

void TFT_SendCommand(uint8_t cmd);
void TFT_SendData(uint8_t data);
void TFT_Init(void);
void TFT_Clear(void);
```

```c
int main(void) {
HAL_Init();
SystemClock_Config();
MX_GPIO_Init();

TFT_Init();
TFT_Clear();

while (1) {

}
}

void SystemClock_Config(void) {
// Configure the system clock as needed
}

static void MX_GPIO_Init(void) {
__HAL_RCC_GPIOB_CLK_ENABLE();

GPIO_InitTypeDef GPIO_InitStruct = {0};
GPIO_InitStruct.Mode =
GPIO_MODE_OUTPUT_PP;
GPIO_InitStruct.Pull = GPIO_NOPULL;
GPIO_InitStruct.Speed = GPIO_SPEED_FREQ_LOW;

GPIO_InitStruct.Pin = TFT_RS_PIN;
HAL_GPIO_Init(TFT_RS_PORT, &GPIO_InitStruct);
```

```c
// Initialize other TFT control and data pins
}

void TFT_SendCommand(uint8_t cmd) {
// Implement sending command to TFT display
using GPIO pins
}

void TFT_SendData(uint8_t data) {
// Implement sending data to TFT display using
GPIO pins
}

void TFT_Init(void) {
// Implement TFT display initialization sequence
using TFT_SendCommand
}

void TFT_Clear(void) {
TFT_SendCommand(0x01); // Clear display
command
HAL_Delay(5); // Delay after clear command
}
```
In this example, you need to implement the
TFT_SendCommand and TFT_SendData functions
to send the appropriate command and data to the
TFT display using the GPIO pins. The TFT_Init

function initializes the TFT display, and the TFT_Clear function clears the display.

Adjust the GPIO pins, initialization sequence, and other settings according to your specific TFT display's requirements.

Please note that TFT displays may have varying initialization sequences and data communication protocols, so you should refer to your TFT display's datasheet and documentation for accurate details and implementation guidelines.

Remember to refer to the TFT display datasheet, STM32 reference manual, and specific STM32CubeIDE documentation for accurate details and implementation guidelines.

# FREE RTOS IN STM32 CUBEIDE TASKS PRIORITIES

The main idea behind our T OS is to perform multiple tasks at the same time. Today, I will show you the benefit of using an OS how to create tasks in free RT OS and how to handle priorities I am using STM 32 Cube ID and I will start by creating a project in cube MX. I am choosing version one because it is supported by majority of the microcontrollers in the setting leave everything as it is make sure that the preemption is enabled we will use preemption based scheduling in which a higher priority task can take control from a lower one you can Google about it go to tasks and queues tab and here you will see a predefined task. Here you will see some details about it its name priority level stack size and tree function. I will explain all these along the project I will create one task here and another one in the program itself I am going to name it as task two its priority will be normal stack sizes 128 and the entry point will be task two in it everything else unchanged and task is created this is it for the free RT O 's part the rest of the setup as usual I am also using you up to show the importance of priority levels let's set the clock for the maximum clock and everything is done click save.

So we got a warning saying that we shouldn't use sis tick with the autos so go to CES and change the time base to any timer I am also using these two pins as output to demonstrate some stuff. Click Save now and code should generate. Open the main dot c file. First I will explain some AR t o s related things. Oh s thread ID stored the unique ID of the thread. All the operations that we will do related to any thread will require this ID. Next the entry points of the thread that we created are defined. These are basically the main functions of the tasks you have to write your task related code in it. Next, inside the main function, the main task is created. First the task is defined and then it is created. Oh s thread def takes the following arguments. The first is the name of the task than the entry point of the task than the priority of the task than the instance and the stack size. Once the task is defined, we need to create it using OS thread CREATE FUNCTION

And after successful creation, the thread ID is stored in the relevant variable that we defined in the beginning of last OS kernel start is called after this point the scheduler will overtake and the control does not reach beside this line. I will demonstrate that in a while. If you scroll down, you will see that the entry points are defined here. Like I said, we have to write our code in these functions. I will do that in few minutes. But let me start by writing the code inside the while loop. So, here I will try to toggle P A zero and P A one after some delay so, compile the code, there are no errors. let's debug it choose STM 32 application, we don't need to modify anything, just choose okay fine, let's run it and see. So as expected, there is no movement on the oscilloscope. Like I mentioned, once the kernel starts, the scheduler takes over and the control doesn't reach the while loop. So I will comment out the line here. So the kernel don't start let's run the program again. Yeah, so we have a wave with time period of around five milliseconds. Actually, what I wanted to do is to generate a wave of one millisecond on pa zero pin and another wave with a period of too many seconds on P A one pin. But obviously it's not going to happen by simply writing in a while loop. So here comes the RT o s in the default task, I am going to toggle the pin PA zero with a period of one millisecond and in the tasks to toggle the pin P A one with a period of two milliseconds at this point shedule a know what I want and it's going to shedule the entire process in a way that every task gets the time they the defined for let's compile and run it. Right now, the pin is connected to PA zero and you can see that the period is one milli second. Now I am switching the pin to PA one and the period changes to two milliseconds. So here both the tasks even with a delay as small as one millisecond can run simultaneously. This is the benefit of using our t o s over a simple programming.

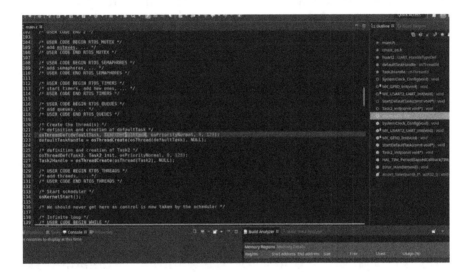

But obviously, this is not it. Let's see the basic most types of problems that we face with the RT O S. Let me explain you the row We'll have priorities now. First, I will define a function to send some data to the UART. This function is supposed to run only in the default task I will define another function to send data to UART. And this one will run in Task Two. Before proceeding any further, I will create another task here. To do so, first we have to create a thread ID for the task, then, we have to create an entry function for the task, I will name it as task three in it. Next, inside the main function, we have to define the thread first. So, oh s thread depth is used. And the parameters will be the name of the task, the entry point of the task, the priority instance and at last the stack size. Then, we will create the thread and assign the ID to the task three handle. And, at last, write some code in the entry function of the task. Make sure that you write everything in a while loop. These tasks are not defined to handle return. So you should always have everything inside an infinite loop. Just like the other two, I am also going to write one UART function for the third task it's time to write our code now. So the default task is going to send the data to the UART every one second. And task two is going to send the data every two seconds. Let's compile this and see how the RT o s handles this situation. As you can see that each task is printing every second. But this is not what we opted for. We wanted the default task to print every second and tasked to to print every two seconds. Let's test this between the default task and the task three, which runs every three seconds. Okay, as you can see, the default task prints twice, and then in the third second, both default and task three prints together. Here the code works all right, because the delay is large. But what if the time delays same for all the tasks. So here, I will use all three tasks to transmit with the same delay of one second. Let's compile the code and debug it. As you can see, even though the data is being transmitted, it's not what we were looking for. Every task waits three seconds to transmit again. But we wanted all of them to transmit every one second.

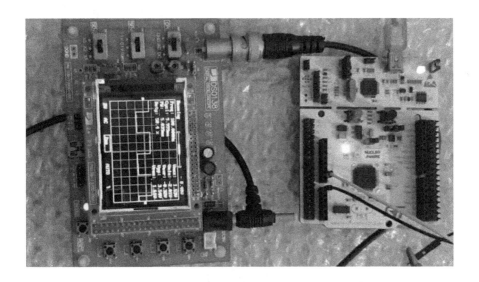

This happens because they all are sharing the same UART. To avoid these situations with the shared resources, we will use the priorities currently, they all have the same priorities. I will change the priority of Task Two to the above normal and the task one two below normal. So finally we have three tasks all with different priorities and sharing the same resource. Let's See what happens now. As you can see now that all three of them are printing at the same time and every one second. This is exactly what we were looking for. Also note that tasked to prints first than default task and at last task three. The reason behind this is the task two priority is highest as it is above normal than default task, which is normal. And at last task three, which is below normal. So they are executed in the same order as their priorities. This is it guys. I hope you understood some basic concepts here. This was just the introduction about what our TOS is on how to handle some basic function in it.

# FREERTOS TASK OPERATIONS STM32 CUBEIDE

We will see the various operations that we can perform on the tasks. Let's start by creating the project and cube Id first I am using STM 32 F 446 or E controller give some name to it and click Finish now, first of all I am going to select the external clock I am using cm CIS version one as it is supported in majority of the STM 32 devices leave everything as it is just enable the V task delay until it's an important parameter and I will explain you how it works in the CIS time based Source Select any source other than cystic I am using timer one.

Next, set up the clock and click Save to generate the project. I am including stdio dot h file because I am going to use the printf to debug we have to define a new write function. I already made a project about printf debugging, check that on the top right corner. First of all let's see if the things are working properly before everything starts. default task is already defined by default. This is to check if the task runs or not giving a delay of one second for this task. Let's build the code in the debug configuration, enable the serial wire viewer in the core clock type the frequency of the HCl K. Now go to Windows Show View as WV and select ITM data console. In the setting enable the comparators zero and check the stimulus port zero press the red button to start recording now you can see the print F string being printed on the console. This means that the default task is running well every one second.

Now let's create another task. To do so, first we need to define the task handler. Next, define the entry function for the task now inside the main function, first of all Find the thread all thread def takes the following parameters name of the Task Entry function for the task priority I am giving it higher priority than the default task instance and stack size Next we need to assign the ID of this task to its handler now I am writing the entry function for this task it will print the value of the index variable and a delay of two seconds let's build it and I will explain you how this works make sure you press the record button Okay, let's see starting is printed at the beginning.

Now the control will be transferred to the colonel the colonel have two tasks in the ready state default task and tasks to the priority of Task Two is higher and that's why it will run first after running the printf statement, the task will go in the BLOCKED state for two seconds. Colonel will now run the default task after executing the printf statement this task will also go into BLOCKED state for one second nothing will run for this one second now after one second default task will again become ready and Colonel will run it after printing the task will again go in the BLOCKED state for one second nothing will run for another second after one second both the tasks will be in ready state again because it's been two seconds since the task two was blocked. The Colonel now again have two tasks ready to run but it will run the task to first because of the higher priority and this whole process will continue again and again. Let's take a look at some other functions

217

available for task management we are going to take a look at OS threads suspend and OS thread resume functions. Both of them take thread ID is the argument of course the thread ID of the thread that you want to suspend or resume if index becomes for the default task should suspend. And if index become seven the default task will resume. Let's run it now. Make sure you enable the record button okay, you see it happened. Now, let me explain what's happening here let's take a look at the task to code you see, when the index was three, it will be printed and the index will increment to four. After this, the task will go in the BLOCKED state for two seconds, when the task resumes after two seconds index have the value of four and control will go inside the if loop the default task will be suspended after that, this loop will not be executed and Ctrl will go back to the beginning where the value of the index will be printed and index will be incremented to five, the task will be blocked for two seconds. As there is no default task anymore, this will keep executing every two seconds, the same thing will happen when the index become seven. The default task will resume this time. So this was the demo for suspend and resume tasks. Let me comment all this. Next, I am going to terminate the task to itself Oh s thread terminate also requires the thread ID as the argument. Let's run this one now.

As you can see here, the task foo gets terminated and default task runs only afterwards. We can also terminate default task just give the thread ID of the same once the task is terminated, it can't be resumed This is the difference between suspend and terminate. We can also suspend all or resume all threads. O S delay until is another function I wanted to show you guys. It blocks the task for some time and resumes automatically. As you can see the description we need to define a variable to store the elapsed time. Again, I'm going to run this under a specific condition and once the condition is reached the task will be blocked for three seconds. Let's run it as you can see the exact thing happening here. The tasking is blocked for three seconds and resumes after that. There are more functions available for tasks and I can't cover all of them. Oh s thread yield passes the control to the next thread that's ready to execute. Again, we can use it under something addition.

# FREERTOS BINARY SEMAPHORE STM32 CMSIS CUBEIDE

I am going to show you guys how to use binary semaphore.

- Semaphores are used to synchronize tasks with other events in the system (especially IRQs)
- Waiting for semaphore is equal to wait() procedure, task is in blocked state not taking CPU time
- Semaphore should be created before usage
- In FreeRTOS implementation semaphores are based on queue mechanism
- In fact those are queues with length 1 and data size 0
- There are following types of semaphores in FreeRTOS:
  - **Binary** – simple on/off mechanism
  - **Counting** – counts multiple *give* and multiple *take*
  - **Mutex** – Mutual Exclusion type semaphores (explained later on)
  - **Recursive** (in CMSIS FreeRTOS used only for Mutexes)
- **Turn on** semaphore = **give** a semaphore can be done from other task or from interrupt subroutine (function `osSemaphoreRelease()` )
- **Turn off** semaphore = **take** a semaphore can be done from the task (function `osSemaphoreWait()` )

So, semaphores are used to synchronize tasks with other tasks or with the interrupts you should create a semaphore before using it a semaphore can be taken or released using the respective functions in free RT OS, the semaphore are four types and they are binary semaphore, counting semaphore mutex and recursive we will cover all of them one by one, we will start with binary semaphore.

Today, I will try to explain the concept of binary semaphore in the simplest possible way, imagine there are three people in a group discussion, they want to talk about their opinion on some topic, if we will allow all of them to speak, there will be some set of problems. First, we won't be able to understand anything second, the loudest person will always take over others opinion. So, to avoid this, we will bring in the talking chair, the person who sits on the chair can speak and others have to just wait for their turn think of the binary semaphore has this chair and the three people as three tasks if a task want to execute it have to acquire the semaphore first binary semaphore simply means that either it can be one or zero. So, either the task have the semaphore or it doesn't, there is no third stage here. Now, the very important part, not having the chair does not mean that the people can't talk of course, they can still speak, but we have to make this rule about the chair. Similarly, if you let a task execute without waiting for the semaphore, it will execute considering it of higher priority. So, to use the semaphore properly, we must always make the task wait for the semaphore and once the task acquires the semaphore it is allowed to run. If all of it sounds complicated to you, don't worry, you will get this during the programming. So, let's start by creating the project in STM 32 Cube IDE, I am using STM 32 F 446 R II controller give a name to the project and click Finish. First of all, I am enabling the external crystal in the SIS option choose the time source other than sis tick I am choosing timer one enable the free RT O 's leave the setup as default we don't need to change anything go to tasks and queues.

Here one default task is already defined, I am going to modify this task its name is going to be normal task priority is going to be normal only stack size as default one I am changing entry function also starts normal task I am creating two more tasks high task with priority above normal and a low task with Priority below normal. Now go to timers and semaphores. Here we are going to create a binary semaphore give some name to it other than this I am enabling you ought to in order to communicate with the computer. Also there is a button connected to PC 13 and therefore it must be selected as input. Now go to the clock setup. I have an eight megahertz crystal on my nucleo board and I want the controller to run at maximum clock possible Click Save and the project will be generated as you can see here, the handlers for all three tasks and the semaphore is defined, we have entry functions for the three tasks here tasks are created inside the main function. And here, we have to write the functions of these tasks. Let's start with high priority task first. As soon as the control enters the high task, this statement will be sent to the UART. And after sending the exit statement, the control will exit the high task, I am just trying to show the working of these tasks first, before we go to the binary semaphore, the same will happen in the medium task.

And same in the low priority task also, I am using 500 milliseconds delay for these tasks. So each task will run once and then go to the suspended state for 500 milliseconds. Let's build the project. There are no errors.

So let's debug the code. Choose STM 32 application and click OK. I am using Hercules for the serial console. Run the program for few seconds. Let's see what do we get. So, at the beginning shedule I have three tasks of different priorities. Therefore, it will run the high priority task first. Here you can see the statements from the high task being printed on this console than the high task will go in the suspend state for 500 milliseconds and the scheduler will run the medium priority task. Similarly, it will run the low task at the end after 500 milliseconds, all three tasks will be available again sheduled will again run them in the same order and this cycle will continue forever. So, the tasks are running properly. Now, I am going to wait for some specific event inside the medium task. So until the pin PC 13 goes low, the medium task is going to wait PC 13 is connected to an input button on board. Let's build this code and see what happens I am going to run it for few seconds. Now, as expected, the higher task runs first and then the control goes in the medium task basically, this instruction has been executed and the medium task is waiting for the button to be pressed. If I do not press the button this instruction will never execute the higher task will resume after 500 milliseconds and preempt the medium task.

```
Leaving HighTask
Entered HighTask
Leaving HighTask
Entered HighTask
Leaving HighTask
Entered HighTask
Leaving HighTask
Entered HighTask
Leaving HighTask
Entered HighTask
Leaving HighTask
Entered HighTask
Leaving HighTask
Entered HighTask
Leaving HighTask
Entered HighTask
Leaving HighTask
Leaving MediumTask
Entered LowTask
Leaving LowTask
Entered HighTask
Leaving HighTask
Entered MediumTask
Entered HighTask
Leaving HighTask
Entered HighTask
Leaving HighTask
Entered HighTask
Leaving HighTask
Entered HighTask
Leaving HighTask
Serial port COM5 closed
```

This will keep happening as the priority of the high task is higher than the medium task. On the other hand, low task cannot preempt the medium task because of lower priority so it will also wait for the medium task to complete. Now once I press the button, the rest of the medium task will run and therefore the control will go inside the low task and back to high task again. It will enter the medium task and wait for the event once again. You can see in the result whenever I am pressing the button the medium task will exit and low task can run As we saw, the higher priority task can preempt the lower priority tasks, even when the low task is running. To avoid this preemption, and to safeguard the shared resources, we use the semaphores. I am just going to modify this statement a little. These are some important functions available for semaphores o s semaphore create creates the semaphore o s semaphore wait waits for the semaphore to become available, the first parameter is the ID of the semaphore handle and the second parameter is the waiting time in milliseconds. If you enter zero, that would mean that it is not going to wait at all, and the execution of the task will continue irrespective of whether it has the semaphore or not o s semaphore release releases the semaphore So, that it becomes available for the other task as the semaphore was already created, when we set up the project at the beginning, I will just start by acquiring the semaphore we have to wait for the semaphore to become available, and we are going to wait forever if the semaphore would be available, this will acquire it this statement would ensure that the semaphore has been acquired and after the task is complete, we are going to release the semaphore.

```
275 void Startnormaltask(void const * argument)
276 {
277   /* USER CODE BEGIN 5 */
278   /* Infinite loop */
279   for(;;)
280   {
281     char *str1 = "Entered MediumTask and waiting for semaphore\n";
282     HAL_UART_Transmit(&huart2, (uint8_t *) str1, strlen (str1), 100);
283
284     osSemaphoreWait(BinSemHandle, osWaitForever);
285
286     while (HAL_GPIO_ReadPin(GPIOC, GPIO_PIN_13));  // wait till the pin go low
287
288     char *str2 = "Leaving MediumTask\n";
289     HAL_UART_Transmit(&huart2, (uint8_t *) str2, strlen (str2), 100);
290     osDelay(500);
291   }
292   /* USER CODE END 5 */
293 }
294
295 /* USER CODE BEGIN Header_Starthightask */
296 /**
297  * @brief Function implementing the HighTask thread.
298  * @param argument: Not used
299  * @retval None
300  */
301 /* USER CODE END Header_Starthightask */
302 void Starthightask(void const * argument)
303 {
304   /* USER CODE BEGIN Starthightask */
305
306   /* Infinite loop */
```

**MEDIUM PRIORITY TA**

I am going to write the same rules in the high priority task and the statements accordingly. So, wait for the semaphore, acquire it and then release the semaphore. On the other hand, let's leave the low priority task as it is just to show that the task can still execute without the need for the semaphores let's debug our code now. Note that I am not stopping the execution this time. So, the high task will run first it will acquire the semaphore and release it the semaphore will become available for the other tasks, the medium task will acquire it now, the medium task will wait for the button to be pressed. The high task will resume from suspension and preempt the medium task it will again try to take the semaphore but the semaphore has been acquired by the medium task and has not been released yet. High task can't continue without the semaphore. So we'd have to wait for it to become available. Now, all three tasks are waiting at this point. So an idle task will be running in the background. Also note that even the low task does not need any semaphore to run, it still can't preempt the medium task and therefore, it has to wait for the medium task to finish its execution. As soon as the button is pressed, the medium task will resume and it will release the semaphore and then go back in the suspension state for 500 milliseconds.

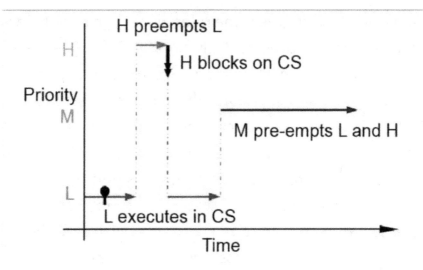

Once the semaphore becomes available, the high task will acquire it and continue its execution from the point it was stopped. After the high task is executed, the low task will run because the medium task is still in the suspended state. Once again the loop continues from high task executing than the medium task acquiring the semaphore high task trying to preempt the medium task, but it has to wait for the semaphore to be released by the medium task. And once the key is pressed, semaphore is released the higher task and the lower task can run. Although the binary semaphore might seems like the perfect solutions for the task operations, it have its own shortcomings. One of those And probably the most important one is priority inversion. priority inversion is pretty simple to understand. When a low priority task preempts the higher priority task, it's called priority inversion. Take this picture for example, let's say the low task is running in some critical section and it have acquired the semaphore. High task also needs to run in their critical sections, and it needs the semaphore to do that. It has to wait obviously, for the semaphore to be released by the low task. Now, if a medium priority task starts running, it can preempt the low task. This way now, the higher priority task have to wait for both the medium and the low task to finish. Even the priority of the high task is highest, it has to wait for the medium task to finish. This scenario is called priority inversion. I will show it in the working state. Let's take the contents of the medium task and replace them with the low task I just need to change these eight votes. Let's build the code and debug it.

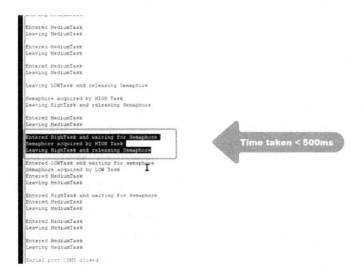

As expected, the higher task will run first, it will acquire and release the semaphore. Next, the medium priority task will run. Now the Ctrl goes in the low task, it will acquire the semaphore and wait for the button to be pressed. Let's call it the critical section. By this time, the higher task will resume and preempt the low task. As the semaphore is still acquired by the low task high task have to wait for it. The medium task will resume and preempt the low task. The medium task does not need any semaphore to run so it will keep executing every 500 milliseconds. Now the important point is even if I press the button below task have to wait for the medium task to finish its execution. This way high task will also have to wait for the medium task to finish and we have a priority inversion scenario here. We will cover the methods to avoid priority inversion in the upcoming projects. Let's continue this execution. Now once the button is pressed, the low task will continue its execution it will release the semaphore and high task will continue from the waiting point. Now the medium task will run again the high task will get the control and it will execute acquiring and releasing semaphore the time it took to do this is of course way less than 500 milliseconds. Because of this the low task will run as the medium task is still suspended and waiting for 500 milliseconds to complete low task will acquire the semaphore and wait for the event medium task will come out of suspension and preempt the low task. At this point, the high task is waiting for its 500 milliseconds of wait period to complete. Now, the high task will resume and try to acquire the semaphore and it has to wait this onward the medium task will keep pre-empting the low task ever 500 milliseconds and the same thing will continue whenever the key is pressed.

# FREERTOS COUNTING SEMAPHORE STM32 NO CMSIS

I am going to walk you through the counting semaphores in free RT O S, like I mentioned in the post, I am not going to use the CM ces API and instead I will be using free RT o s functions directly. If you want to browse more projects on our t o s, you can check out the playlist on the top right corner. Let's start by creating the project in STM 32 Cube ID I am using a 446 r e give the name to the project and click Finish this is the cube MX and let's begin the setup I am selecting the external crystal for the clock let's enable the free r t o s enabled to use the counting semaphore leave everything as it is a default task will be created and we can't remove it from here Next select the time based source anything other than cystic I am enabling you off to an interrupt mode to communicate with the PC.

Let's set up the clock now. I have eight megahertz crystal on the board and I want the controller to run at maximum possible clock click Save to generate the project here is the main dot c file. First, let's open the CM sis dot h file. I am going to include all these directly to my project. Although I don't need all of them, I am including just in case comment out the CM sis file.

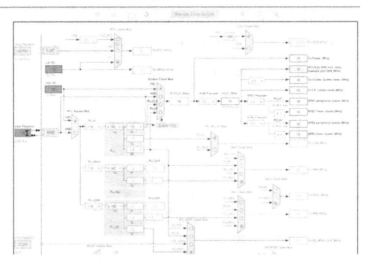

Now we are not going to use any of the CM sis function here I need to include few more files that is STD lib and string dot h you will see their usage in a while I am removing the default task related functions that were created by default. Let's start the process by defining the task related functions first. Here HPT handler will be the handler for the high priority task and HPT task is the entry function where the task code will be written. In the same way, I am creating three more handlers for the medium priority task, low priority task and very low priority task.

```
68  /* USER CODE BEGIN PFP */
69
70  /* USER CODE END PFP */
71
72 /* Private user code ---------------------------------
73  /* USER CODE BEGIN 0 */
74
75  // create task defines
76
77  TaskHandle_t HPThandler;
78  void HPT_TASK (void *pvParameters);
79
80  TaskHandle_t MPThandler;
81  void MPT_TASK (void *pvParameters);
82
83  TaskHandle_t LPThandler;
84  void LPT_TASK (void *pvParameters);
85
86  TaskHandle_t VLPThandler;
87  void VLPT_TASK (void *pvParameters);
88
89  se
90
91  /* USER CODE END 0 */
92
93 /**
94   * @brief  The application entry point.
95   * @retval int
96   */
97 int main(void)
98 {
99    /* USER CODE BEGIN 1 */
100
101   /* USER CODE END 1 */
102
103
104      /* MCU Configuration------------------------------
```

Next, we need to create a handler for the semaphore. I am naming it counting Sam. Now I am creating a resource which have three values and some other variables that are going to be used. Our x data is going to store the value received from you art First we need to create the

semaphore X semaphore create counting takes two
parameters, first is the maximum number of counts you
want and second is the initial count value, I am creating
the semaphore with three tokens, because the resource
have three values and three tasks can access it
simultaneously.

```
119
120    /* Configure the system clock */
121    SystemClock_Config();
122
123    /* USER CODE BEGIN SysInit */
124
125    /* USER CODE END SysInit */
126
127    /* Initialize all configured peripherals */
128    MX_GPIO_Init();
129    MX_USART2_UART_Init();
130    /* USER CODE BEGIN 2 */
131
132    HAL_UART_Receive_IT(&huart2, &rx_data, 1);
133
134    CountingSem = xSemaphoreCreateCounting(3,0);
135    if (CountingSem == NULL) HAL_UART_Transmit(&huart2, (uint8_t *) "Unable to Create Semaphore\n\n", 28, 100);
136    else HAL_UART_Transmit(&huart2, (uint8_t *) "Counting Semaphore created successfully\n\n", 41, 1000);
137
138
139    // create TASKS
140
141    xTaskCreate(HPT_TASK, "HPT", 128, NULL, 3, &HPThandler);
142    xTaskCreate(MPT_TASK, "MPT", 178, NULL, 2, &MPThandler);
143    xTaskCreate(LPT_TASK, "LPT", 128, NULL, 1, &LPThandler);
144    xTaskCreate(VLPT_TASK, "VLPT", 128, NULL, 0, &VLPThandler);
145
146    vTaskStartScheduler();
147
148    /* USER CODE END 2 */
149
150
151    /* We should never get here as control is now taken by the scheduler */
152
153    /* Infinite loop */
154    /* USER CODE BEGIN WHILE */
```

If the semaphore is created the handler that is counting
CEM will have any other value than Now next, we need to
create the tasks X task creates takes the following
parameters. First is the task code or entry function, the
name stack size task parameter priority and the handlers
address you can give any name to these tasks name is not
used anywhere in the program. Similarly, I have created
three more tasks with different priorities based on their
names. And finally, we will start the scheduler. Now, we
have to write the tasks I will start with high priority tasks

first. It's going to print this string when the control enters the task. Now, we will take the semaphore X semaphore Tech have two arguments first is the semaphore handler and waiting time port max delay means it's going to wait forever for the semaphore to become available. If the semaphore is acquired successfully, these statements will be executed i t o Oh A is the function to convert integer to the string first parameters is the integer value than the character array and then the format type. After this I am joining all these strings and finally send it to the UART increment the index variable and added a delay of three seconds in the beginning of the task, let's release three semaphores so, that three tasks can acquire them. medium priority task is also going to be same other than releasing semaphore. One of the very important property of counting semaphore is that you can release the semaphore at any point in the code. Unlike binary semaphore, it's not necessary to release the semaphore by the task which have acquired it so, I have created four tasks with different wait time. Let's build the code there are no errors so, flash it to the board I am using Hercules for the serial monitor let's put breakpoints inside each task okay let's run the program. As expected, the HVT will run first and hit the breakpoint counting semaphore was created and the statement from HP T. Note that at this point there are three tokens available as we release them while entering the HPT. semaphore was acquired data was accessed and HPT was suspended for three seconds.

semaphore wasn't released by the HPT. So there are two tokens available at this point. Now the NPT runs accesses data and goes into suspension without releasing the semaphore. Token available is one lp t runs, accesses the data and goes into suspension without releasing the semaphore again, tokens available as zero control have entered the VLP t. Let's see what happens now, the LPT couldn't get the semaphore because there is no token available now LPT will come out of suspension in one second and preempt the LPT and it will try to take the semaphore as there is no semaphore token available, all these tasks will go in the waiting forever states. Next, let's set the URL to receive one byte of data in the interrupt mode. Once the interrupt is triggered, a callback function will be called and we must write that too. If the received data is ah, we will release the semaphore here. Releasing the semaphore from ISR is not that straightforward? First, we must create a variable called higher priority task Wolken and initialize it with P D false. Then we have to release the semaphore using x semaphore gift from ISR whose parameter will the address of the variable that we created just now along with the handler. The idea behind this is let's say the interrupt was triggered when the control was in LPT. While the interrupt is being processed, the higher priority task preempted the lower priority. Now, when the ISR exits, the control shouldn't go back to the lower task and therefore high priority task Wolken parameter will be automatically set through Port N switch will do the context switch if the variable is true. If the variable is false, the port N switch have no effect. You must write this in every ISR function let's not give these semaphores at the beginning also I am going to modify the tasks a bit. Instead of suspending they will be deleted at the end passing no means delete the current task the LPT won't delete but it will keep going in the suspension. Let's build the code and flash it to the board I forgot to stop the reception in the callback function. We skipped the breakpoints. Let's see. semaphore created successfully HPT runs but couldn't get the semaphore because there is none available. Same for the MPT LPT and VIP t all tasks are waiting for the semaphore token to become available. Now let's add the character our from PC to the controller. As you see on receiving our the semaphore was released and the HBT resumes and delete itself. Again, MPT resumes and deletes itself LPT resumes and delete, now, only the LPT is left and it will keep resuming every 500 milliseconds. Let's take a look at the another important function in the free rt OSUXM A forget count gives the number of available tokens of the counting semaphore, I am again using Ito a to convert the number to the string and I am going to release the semaphores in the beginning I am using same setup for the other tasks also. Let's build and run the code now. So, HBT task runs and there are three token available right now, the number of tokens decreases because the tasks are not releasing the semaphore when the VLP T runs, there is not token available and therefore, it will wait for it forever when we send the character are the semaphore get released and the VLP T runs and again go into the suspension till the next token become available let's not delete the tasks and keep them under suspended states. I am going to release three semaphores from the ISR if the character R is received let's debug the code at the beginning three semaphores were released the number of tokens available decreases when there is no token available every task will be waiting for the semaphore.

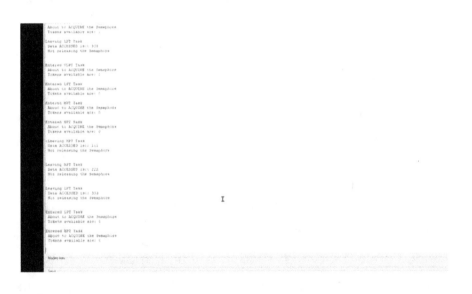

When the character R is sent three tokens will be released and the three top priority tasks will run again these tasks will go in the waiting state for the semaphore and same thing will happen again if I send the character notes that only the task HPT NPT and LPT runs this is because the VLP T task get preempted while waiting for the semaphore This is it about the counting semaphore. You can implement it according to your requirement. Remember that counting semaphore can be released from anywhere in the code irrespective of the task holding it. Those who liked to have theme like this go to Eclipse market place click popular this is the theme I am using darkest dark theme.

# FREERTOS SIMPLE QUEUE STM32 NO CMSIS CUBEIDE

I will start with the simple queue. Let's say we have a queue to hold five integers. Task A is a sender Task and Task B is receiver task. Task A sends an integer to the queue. As the queue is empty, the data will acquire the first place when task A sends another data and it will occupy the second place. If the receiver Task B reads the data from the queue, it will read from the head of the queue once the data is read, it will be removed from the queue and all the contents in the queue will shift right this is how the queue works at the basic level.

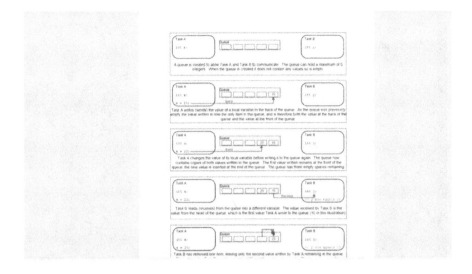

Let's start by creating a project in cube Id first I am using STM 32 F 446 r e give some name to the project and click Finish I am selecting external clock for the MCU selects a time based source anything other than cystic here I am using timer six you off to is to communicate with the computer enable the free RT OS version one leave everything default we have one default task created here let's go to the clock setup.

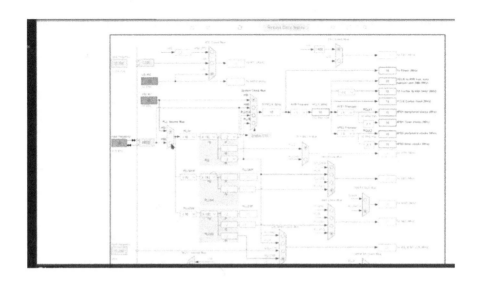

Now. I have eight megahertz crystal on my board H S E means that we are taking input from external crystal I want the MCU to run at maximum clock the setup is done just save it so that the code can be generated I am not going to use the CM sis related functions. That's why we need to manually include all the RT OS related files. These are already present inside the folder we just need to include them in our code we can remove the CM sis Now, other than these I am including string dot h for the string related operations let's remove all the default task related functions which were generated by default. We have to define the task handlers first. There are going to be two sender tasks and one receiver task. Next, we need to define the queue handler. I am naming it simple queue. These are the task functions where the task code will be written inside the main function. First of all we need to create the QX que creo takes two parameters. First is the length of the queue, this queue can hold up to five elements. And next is the size of each element I want the queue to hold the integer elements, that's why integer size if there is some error while the creation of the queue it will return zero and we will display this string on the console if the queue was created successfully, it will return anything other than zero and in that case, we will display this string Next, we need to create three tasks X task create takes the following parameters the task code that we define here some name for the task stack size, the parameter that you want to pass to the task priority of this task. And last is the handler for this task. This is a high priority task. So I have given a priority of three to it. In the same way I am going to create a low priority task with the priority of two but this time I am going to pass some parameter to this task. If you take a look at the definition of exe tasks create the parameter is of type void pointer. That's what we need to pass into this task.

So I am sending a void pointer to this number. Next, we will create a receiver task with the least priority of one. This is to receive serial data from the computer in interrupt mode, I still need to define the RX data and at last we are going to start the scheduler. Here is the high priority send a task this number will be sent to the queue to convert the milliseconds into the ticks. When the control enters HP T this string will be sent via UART. Then we will send the data into the queue XQ send takes the following parameters. The first is the queue handler. Next is the address of the data that you want to send. And last is the text to wait before the timeout occurs. I am sending this number to the queue and I want the task to wait forever for the space to become available in case the queue is full. If the data is sent successfully, it will return PD pass and we will print this on the console then the task will go into suspension for two seconds. Next is the lower priority send a task. Remember that I passed a number as the parameter while the task was created. To send will get the value from the person limiter we will store the value in the to send variable. Next, this string will be printed on the serial console to indicate that the control has entered the LPT task. Next, the number will be sent to the queue. If the queue is full, the task will wait forever for the space to become available then the task will go into the suspension next is the function for the receiver task. First I have created a variable to save the data we are going to send this string to the console.

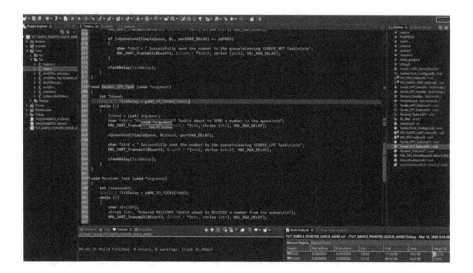

Next we are going to read the data from the queue XQ receive takes the following parameters the handler to the queue, the variable where the data must be saved the number of ticks to wait for the data to become available in case the queue is empty. If there is some error in receiving data, it will not return return PD true and we can display this string then or else the data received will be sent to the console. After this, the receiver task will go into the suspension for five seconds let's build this code there seems to be some error about s print F I forgot to include the library for that let's build the code and debug it. I am using Hercules for the serial communication. I am letting it run for some time. Let's pause it now. So the integer queue was created successfully. Now when the scheduler runs, the control will first go to the high priority task. It's a send a task and it will send 220 tune to the queue. You can see the current queue status on the right. After leaving high priority task, the control will enter the low priority send a task. I will also send the number 111 to the queue and the number will be copied as shown in the picture. Next, the receiver task will run and it will read one data item from the queue. The data read is 222. As you can see in the console. Also, the items in the queue will shift to the right. And you can see the updated queue on the right. Now, after one seconds LPT task will wake up and sends 111 to the queue. Now, after another one second, both HBT and LPT will wake up but HPT will run first and they both will send the respective numbers to the queue. Again after one second LPT wakes up and write 111 to the queue. Now the queue is full. And when HBT wakes up, it's not able to write the data into the queue and so it will be blocked until some space is available in the queue. same will happen For the lower task, now, when the receiver task runs, it will read and remove one item from the queue. One space will be available in the queue high priority task will preempt the receiver task and write the data into the queue and go into suspension for two seconds. Control will reenter the receiver task and it will execute rest of the task, it will print the number received from the queue and go into suspension for five seconds. Now, the high priority task will run and it will try to write the number into the queue. As the queue is full, it will go into the BLOCKED state. Five seconds later, when the receiver task wakes up. Same thing happens again and it will keep happening. Next, we will see how can we send the data into the queue from the interrupt service routine. I am writing the receive callback function for the UART. This is the number that I am going to send to the queue. If the data received his arm, we must first define the high priority task woken to false. I am sending data using XQ center front from my Sr. This will send the data to the front of the queue. The parameters of this function are queue handler, the data to be sent and the high priority task woken note that there is no waiting period. If the queue is full, this function will simply timeout and at last, we must call the port end switching ISR. If the high priority task woken was set true, this will do the context switching looks like there is some warning. We have to pass the address of this variable here. All is good. Now let's debug our code. I have sent the character R and we can see the string also printed here. Let's see what happened here in each step. Integer queues created high priority task runs and write the number into the queue LPT runs and write another number receive the task reads and removes the first number from the queue. Again LPT runs and writes another number to the queue. It will keep going on until the data are is received from the UART the number 123456789 is sent to the front of the queue and the rest of the items will shift back.

When the control enters the receiver task, it will read this number as it's the first number in the queue. After reading, the number will be removed from the queue and rest of the processing of the queue will continue in the usual order. In this project, we saw how to create integer queue and how to pass data between the tasks using this queue.

# FREERTOS STRUCTURED QUEUE MEMORY ALLOCATION STM32

free RT OS I covered how to send or receive data using queue a queue can only hold the data of same type if we want to transfer the data of different types we have to use structure queue and in this project we are going to discuss about it we will start by creating the project in cube ID select the controller you are using give some name to the project and click Finish in the cube MX first of all I am selecting external crystal for the clock go to CES and select the time base anything other than cystic I am selecting timer six you off to is to communicate with the computer select the free RT OS version one and leave everything as it is this default task will be created and we will deal with it later.

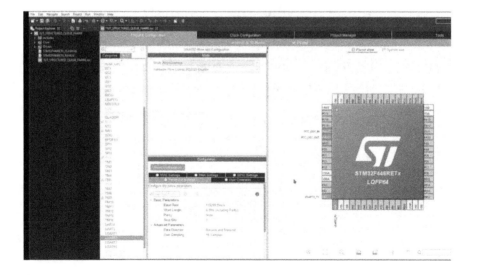

Now go to the clock setup the crystal is eight megahertz and I want the controller to run at 180 megahertz click Save to generate the project I am not going to use the CM sis API. So go to cm sis dot h file and copy all these we will include them directly in our project comment at the CM sis file, we will remove the default task related functions which were generated by default. Let's start with the coding now. First to define the cue handler Next, we need to define the task handlers I will be using to send the tasks and one receiver task like I said in the beginning that we will be sending different data types to the same queue. To do that, we need to create a structure of all those data types. I am creating this structure which have a pointer to the character an integer and an unsigned 16 bit integer. Let's call it my struct these will be required to inside the main function, we first need to create a queue that can hold the structure type. This Q can store two elements which are of the type my struct. These string will be printed based on if the queue was created or not. After creating queue, we will create the tasks looks like I forgot To define the task functions, let's define them now these functions are where the task related code will be written.

```
115     /* USER CODE BEGIN SysInit */
116
117     /* USER CODE END SysInit */
118
119     /* Initialize all configured peripherals */
120     MX_GPIO_Init();
121     MX_USART2_UART_Init();
122     /* USER CODE BEGIN 2 */
123
124     /***** create QUEUE *****/
125     St_Queue_Handler = xQueueCreate(2, sizeof (my_struct));
126
127     if (St_Queue_Handler == 0) // If there is some error while creating qu
128
129     /* USER CODE END 2 */
130
131
132     /* We should never get here as control is now taken by the scheduler */
133     /* Infinite loop */
134     /* USER CODE BEGIN WHILE */
135     while (1)
136     {
137         /* USER CODE END WHILE */
138
139         /* USER CODE BEGIN 3 */
140     }
141     /* USER CODE END 3 */
142 }
143
144 /**
145   * @brief System Clock Configuration
146   * @retval None
147   */
148 void SystemClock_Config(void){
192
```

Next task create takes the following parameters task
function, some name of the task stack depth, the
parameter to the task, the priority of this task and the
handler of this task. Note that I am using same priority of
two for both the sender tasks receive a task have lower
priority after creating the tasks, we will start the
scheduler now, let's write the codes for these tasks. First,
the sender one task I am declaring a pointer to my struct.
This is to convert the delay to tics. When the control
enters the task, this string will be printed on the console.

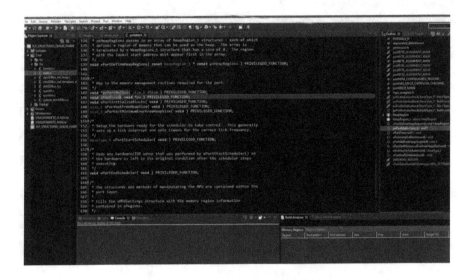

Now, before assigning the data, we must allocate the memory for this pointer to the structure. To do so, we will use P V port malloc function it's defined in the portable dot h file its takes size as the parameter there is also V port free to free the allocated memory I am guessing you are already familiar with the malloc function PV port malloc is also the same, but you can consider it as safer when using the free RT O 's the size of memory we need is same as the size of my struct. Now we will load the data to the structure and then send this data to the queue. XQ send takes the following parameters the handler of the queue the address of the data and the amount of time to wait if the queue is full. If the data is successfully sent to queue, it will return PD pass and this string will be printed to the console let's make it a bit more interesting index one will be incremented by one each time the control enters this task these values will be modified based on this index one value and at last this task will go into suspension for two seconds. Similarly send a task to will also send the data to the queue every two seconds now let's write the receiver task. PTR to struct is another pointer to my struct. This is where the received data will be stored converting three seconds to ticks. This string will be printed when the control enters the receiver task. Now we will receive the data from the queue XQ receive takes the following parameters the handler of the queue address of the variable where the data should be stored and the wait time in case the queue is empty. It will return PD pass if the data is received from the queue. Here we will allocate new memory locations To store the string, I am expecting the size of string could be 100 bytes. Whenever you are using s print F in the free RT OS make sure you allocate the memory like this otherwise s printf will cause hard fall to error this string will be stored in the PTR pointer location.

And we will send this string to the UART after sending free the location of the PTR that we just created, we must also free the memory that we allocated in both the sender tasks. So, we will use V port free and the argument will be the PTR to struct this way the memory will be free for the pointer which was received by the queue and the other pointer will be safe. I will demonstrate this in a while we also need to include the stdio for the S printf and string dot h for the string related functions. Let's build this code now, there are no errors. So, we will debug the code I am using Hercules for the serial console let's run this now, I am going to let it run for a while. So, the queue was created successfully it entered the sender to task sent the data to the queue and task got suspended. Somehow the data is not printing properly here. So, we will just look at the received data. Data from sender one is printed data from sender to again from sender one with new counter value of two and large value increased. Same result from the sender to task let's run it freely. As you can see, the values are printing from both the tasks also the counter is increasing and so is the large value send a one send a two. Now let's see how the memory allocation works reset the debugger I will put a breakpoint here and here and here. notes that I am watching this in the Variables tab and not in the live expression. We hit the first breakpoint. Keep an eye at the PTR to struct it's showing zero right now. When I stepped over this function, memory gets allocated for the PTR to struct. The location for this memory is he plus 1964 we will just consider it as 1964. Let's run the code again. We hit another breakpoint in send a to task. Step eight Over the memory PTR to structure is now 1988. Now we hit the breakpoint in the receiver task. Note the PTR variable the memory allocated for it is 2012. Also a PTR to struct have the data from memory 1964 which is associated with Sen one PTR, two struct right now let's set another breakpoint here, we have already freed the memory of ptr. So 2012 location is free now. If we step over this sender, one PTR, two struct is also free now. If we run the code now we hit the sender one breakpoint again, as the memory 1964 was free, it will be allocated to send a one again let's run it, we hit the sender to break point the memory 1988 is already occupied and next free slot is 2012. Here 2012 will be allocated for the sender to PTR two struct guys, this is just the memory allocation as the queue already have two waiting elements. So sender two can't send the data to the queue right now. We are in the receiver task right now.

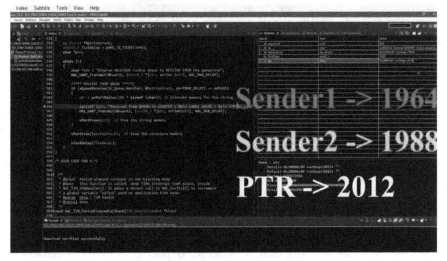

notes that are PTR to struct have the data from the memory location of 1988 which was allocated to sender to task before PTR was allocated the memory of 2036 and was freed in the previous step. After running this statement, memory location of 1988 which was associated with the sender to task is also freed. Again, we are in the center one task the lowest slot available right now is 1988 and this will be allocated to the sender one PTR two struct This is how the memory allocation works. As I mentioned we free the memory after receiving the data and this way only the memory allocated to the point of that we received gets free and other data remains safe.

# FREERTOS MUTEX STM32 CUBEIDE

We will see how to use mutex in a very simple way, this is part one of the project and it will only cover the basics of mutex.

At basic level mutex is very similar to binary semaphore, you can check out my project on binary semaphore maybe that will help you better understand the mutex also let's start by creating a project in cube Id first type the name for the project and click finish here is the cube MX first I am enabling the external crystal for the clock as we are using free RT OS we must select the time base other than cystic enable the UART to communicate with computer enable the free RT OS version one I am leaving everything as it is here this task will be created by default.

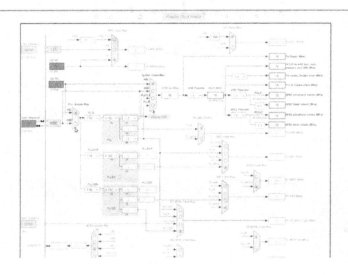

Let's see the clock set up now select the external crystal which is of eight megahertz and I want the system to run at 100 megahertz click Save to generate the code as I am not going to use the CM ces functions copy all these and we will include them in our project separately. Other than these we also need string dot h file we don't need these right now. Also cm sis dot h is not required I am removing the default task related functions Let's begin now first of all we need to define the mutex handler let's call it simple mutex Next, define the task handlers also I am going to use three tasks next, the functions where the task code will be written.

Now, first we will create the mutex using x semaphore create a mutex if the mutex was created successfully, it will return any value other than null and in that case, we will print this string now we will create the tasks X task create takes the following parameters task code where the task code is written name of the task stack size parameter the priority and the handler I am assigning a priority of three to the HP T and lower priorities for the other tasks. Now start the scheduler. We don't need all three tasks for this case right now. Now we will write the task related code this string will be printed when the control enters the HP T task Let's create a function which will act as a critical section for this tutorial.

That's why before performing any operations, we need to take the mutex first using x semaphore take function whose parameters are the handler of the semaphore or mutex. And the time for which the function will wait in case the mutex is not available. Once the mutex is acquired, the string will be sent to the UART and then we will release the mutex. Let's set a delay of two seconds here, so that we can better understand the blocking part we will send this string to the UART and we will call that function here after the control comes back from the function, this string will be printed to indicate the end of the task. And finally, this task will suspend for 1500 milliseconds. Same code is written for the medium priority task also just some minor changes let's build it now. We got some warning about the data types. Let's leave it and debug our code. Kay, I am using Hercules for the serial console let's set the breakpoints at these locations. This is to check the flow of the control let's run it now. Obviously, the control will enter the higher task first you can see the string is printed on the console. Now the call to the function sends you out the string got printed successfully H P T acquire the mutex printed the string and released the mutex the HP T task goes into suspension for 1500 milliseconds. The control entered the medium priority task now the entry string is printed here. Now the call to the function sends you art the MPT string was printed and the function will wait for the two seconds delay to complete before releasing the semaphore. By then, the HPT task will wake up and preempt the MPT it will print the entry string and try to take the mutex but the mutex is still held by the NPT.

So the higher task have to wait for the mutex to become available. Once it does the HPT will take the mutex print the string and release the mutex H P T will exit now. The control will go back to MPT and it will also exit same thing will happen if we run the code again. And this cycle will continue if we let it run freely. This is how mutex works. It's basically a mutual exclusion from accessing the same resource by many tasks. If you know about binary semaphore, this is exactly how binary semaphore works to although there is a small difference between them and it's about priority inversion and priority inheritance.

# FREERTOS MUTEX VS BIN SEMAPHORE PRIORITY INVERSION PRIORITY INHERITANCE

I will advise you to do that first. Well, let's resume from where we left off, I will open my last project. Let's uncomment this task.

Now we need all three tasks. In this project, we will see the difference between binary semaphore and mutex. So, let's create a binary semaphore first of all, we need to create the semaphore handler and let's call it bin semaphore. In this function instead of taking mutex we will acquire the binary semaphore I will change this delay position and increase it to five seconds now, just likely create the mutex we will create the binary semaphore also if the semaphore gets created successfully, we will print this string after creating binary semaphore, it must be first given before taking it let's make some small changes in the higher task and the lower priority task I will create a new medium priority task this task will print this string and it does not need any semaphore or mutex to execute and I am giving it the highest suspension time let's build this code few warnings are there we will debug the code now.

let the program run for a while I will explain what is going on here Okay, let's see now, the semaphore and mutex both are created. The high priority task will run first acquire the semaphore, print the string release the semaphore and exit. The medium priority task doesn't need semaphore so it will run normally. Now the Ctrl enters the low priority task, it will call the function send you out and we'll wait for five seconds to complete. But by then high task will wake up and it will also call the send you our function if we will try to acquire the semaphore which is held by the low task higher task have no other option but to wait for the semaphore to become available.

Now, both high and low tasks are waiting, medium task will wake up and run as it doesn't need any semaphore it will continue to run every two seconds. Now think of a situation where those five seconds are over and low task wants to execute. But it can't because the medium task is still running the high task which was already waiting for the low task to release the semaphore now also have to wait for the medium task to finish its execution. So high tasks have to wait for the medium task and this scenario eo is called priority inversion once the medium task finishes low tasks can execute further and release the semaphore. Hi task will acquire the semaphore print the string and exit again the MP T will run and finally, the low task will exit this whole sequence will continue in the similar way forever, I hope you understood the priority inversion properly I will take a picture of this to compare with the mutex output. Now, let's see how to avoid this priority inversion using mutex I am going to change the semaphore with new texts and rest of the code will remain same let's build and debug this now let the program run for a while. Okay, let's see, I will open the picture from the semaphore to compare it with the mutex.

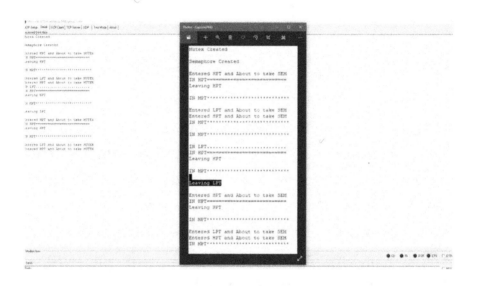

The initial part is same in both of them, control enters the high task, acquire the mutex print the string release the mutex and exit the task medium task will run it doesn't need mutex low task will run and it will acquire the mutex just like as it acquired the semaphore in the other case now, there will be a five seconds delay high task will wake and try to acquire the mutex. Now is the important part as the high task is waiting for the mutex and the low task have the mutex the priority of the low task will change to that of the high task. This scenario is called the priority inheritance because the low task inherited the priority of the highest task waiting for the mutex. Now the medium task cannot preempt this low task because the low task has the highest priority now. This was not the case with semaphore and medium task preempted the low task in that now once the low task releases the mutex high task will acquire it print the string releases it and exit itself the medium task and finally run now and at last low task will also exit basically both the output are same, except the medium task can't preempt the low task in the mutex. And that's because the low task inherits the priority of the highest waiting task which is higher than the medium task. The same sequence will run forever. So this is what priority inversion means. And this is how it is corrected by using priority inheritance.

# FREERTOS SOFTWARE TIMERS STM32 WOCMSIS

The first part will cover the usage of timers using the CM ces functions. And in the second part, I will use the pure free RT o s functions, you can check the timing for the respective parts in the description of the project. The first half of the project where the setup will be done is common for both the parts. Let's start by creating the project in cube Id first, I am using STM 32 F 446 r e controller give the name to the project and click Finish in the cube MX I am enabling the external crystal for the clock. Now before we go into timers, I will explain about them a little.

**One-shot timers versus auto-reload timers**

There are two types of timer, one-shot timers, and auto-reload timers. Once started, a one-shot timer will execute its callback function only once. It can be manually re-started, but will not automatically re-start itself. Conversely, once started, an auto-reload timer will automatically re-start itself after each execution of its callback function, resulting in periodic callback execution.

The difference in behaviour between a one-shot timer and an auto-reload timer is demonstrated by the timeline in the diagram below. In this diagram, Timer 1 is a one-shot timer that has a period equal to 100, and Timer 2 is an auto-reload timer that has a period equal to 200.

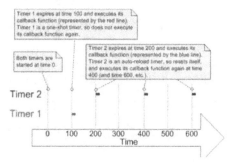

So basically there are two types of timers in free r t o s, auto reload timer and the one shot timer. Once started, a one shot timer will execute its callback function only once it can be manually restarted but will not automatically restart itself. Conversely, an auto reload timer will automatically restart itself after each execution of its callback function resulting in periodic callback execution now let's enable the free RT O 's. In the parameter set up enable the timers usage timer priorities can vary between zero to six keep it at six so that we don't have any problems regarding something pre empting it leave everything as it is for now. If you are watching this project for pure RT OS functions, then you don't need to do any other setup for the free RT O 's. The remaining setup for the free RT O S is only for those who wants to use the CRM says functions go to tasks here you can see the default task is already created. Let's give it some better name. I will call it you off task priority normal is fine task function will also be used to task so we can't have same names for both It's okay now let's create another task. This will be led task I am keeping the priority same as the UAV task so that they don't interfere with each other's operations task function will also be the LED task the tasks part is done here let's create the timer now. I am naming it periodic timer the callback function will be p t callback here you can select the type I am keeping this one is periodic let's create another timer now I couldn't came up with any better name for this one.

Anyway, this will be a one shot timer other parameters are kept as it is and this completes our free RT OS setup. I have pa Five connected to the onboard LED and that's why I am setting it as output also the user button is connected to the pin PC 13 And that's why I am setting it as input now enable the UART so that we can send some data to the computer and also since we are using free RT O S, we need to change time base from SIS tick to any other source. Let's see the clock setup now. I have eight megahertz clock and I want the system to run at 180 megahertz This is it for the setup click Save to generate the project so this is our main file. Here are the task handles and the timer handles. Then we have the task functions and the timer callback defined here inside the main function, first of all the timer is created here is the name of the timer and here is the type the callback is declared in the timer's definition the next part is where the tasks are created. We have already discussed about them in the previous projects now here is the function that will be executed when the UART task will be called. As you must have noticed that we haven't started the timers yet we have only created them. So here when the control enters the UART task, first thing we are going to do is start the periodic timer. I am writing this outside the infinite loop so that it can only run once. Oh s timer stop takes two parameters. The first one is the handle to the timer that you want to start and the second is the time duration for the timer. This timer will expire every one second. Now we will send some data via the UART. And this task will keep running every two seconds. The periodic timer will timeout in one second, and the callback function will be called. In this callback function, we will send another string via the UART indicating that the string is sent from the callback function. Before writing the LED task, let me explain its purpose. So basically, if the button is pressed, the onboard LED should turn on for some particular amount of time.

This will be an implementation of timeout feature for the LED we will first check if the button is pressed. If it is then turn on the LED by pulling the respective pin too high and now we will start the one shot timer for the period of four seconds. In case you want to change the period of the timer during the runtime you have to call the timer start function with the new time period. Note that the timer start function also acts as a timer reset function. So if the timer start is called before the timer is expired, it will reset the timer again. In simpler terms, if the button is pressed before the LED timeout, it will extend the timeout by another time or period Once the timer is expired, the callback function will be called. And here we will turn off the LED let's build this now we have few warnings and they are because of the data types there. I will leave them for now. Next Steve buckets I am using Hercules to monitor the UART data let's run it now as you can see the timer string is printing every one second and on the other hand you are string is printing every two seconds let's press the button the controller the LED turned on and it turned off after four seconds just as we programmed but if we press the button before the timeout, the LED will never turns off.

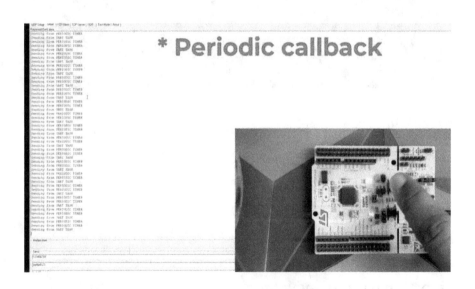

* Periodic callback

You can see the UOP task and the periodic tasks are performing just fine and they are not affected by other tasks and timers This is it for this project. I hope you understood the usage of timers in free RT OS using the CM sis functions you can download the code from the link in the description next half of this project will cover the same but by using the pure RT o s functions I am assuming you have already gone through the setup in the first part of this project. So first of all we need to copy all the header files from cm sis file and paste them in our main file now delete all the pre generated cm sis functions now let's start by creating timer handles. PT handle is for periodic timer and O T handle is for one shot timer now we will create task handles you can see the handles for the uafs task and the LED task now we will write the task functions. Let's start with you our task when the control enters the UOP task, first thing we are going to do is start the periodic timer. I am writing this outside the infinite loop so that it can only run once since the timer is periodic anyway, X timer start takes two parameters. First is the handle of the timer and second is the time to wait before starting the timer. Since we want the timer to start immediately, I am writing a zero here. Now we will send some string via the UART. And this task will keep running every two seconds. p d m s to ticks basically converts the milliseconds to ticks as per the free RT o s setup. This completes the UART task function. Let's write the LED task function now. Before writing the LED task, let me explain its purpose. So basically, if the button is pressed, the onboard LED should turn on for some particular amount of time. This will be an implementation of timeout feature for the LED we will first check If the button is pressed if it is then turn on the LED by pulling the respective pin too high and now we will start the one shot timer immediately the period for the timers is set during their creation, the LED task will run every 20 milliseconds this completes the code for the task related functions. Once the timer is expired, the timer callback functions will be called. And that's why we need to write a callback function now, we can write a common callback for the timers and that's what I am going to do. Let's call it timer callback, and its parameter will be the timer handle. If the callback was called by the periodic timer, we will send this string to the UART. And if it is called by the one shot timer, then the LED will turn off. Note that the timer start function also acts as a timer reset function. So if the timer start is called before the timer is expired, it will reset the timer again. In simpler terms, if the button is pressed before the LED timeout, it will extend the timeout by another timer period. Now let's write our main function. We are going to start with creating the timers X timer create takes the following parameters the name of the timer, he can give some random name as it doesn't matter. Second is the timer period, and I am keeping it one second for the periodic timer. The third parameter is to set if the timer is periodic, or the one shot timer. True means periodic and false means one shot fourth parameter is the timer ID and you can assign any ID to this timer fifth parameter is the callback function for the timer similarly, we will create another timer with minor changes in the parameters of course, this will expire in four seconds. It's not a periodic timer, so P D false and give a different timer ID we also need to equate them to their respective handles since the X timer create function returns the timer handle on success. This is all for timers now let's create the tasks X task create takes the following parameters first is the task function the name of the task again the name does not matter. So use whatever you want. Next is the stack size and I am keeping it 128 Since it was set in the cube MX also next is the parameters which we will keep as null then the priority which I will use as one for the normal priority and the last is the handle for the task. Similarly create the LED task also. This completes the task creation now in the end stop the scheduler let's build it now. We have two warnings here and we can remove them by changing the data types. Okay, we are all set now let's run this program I am using Hercules to monitor the UART data. You can see the timer string is printing every one second and on the other hand you are string is printing every two seconds Let's press the button on the controller the LED turned on and it turned off after four seconds just as we programmed but if we press the button before the timeout, the LED will never turn off. You can see the UOC task and the periodic tasks are performing just fine and they are unaffected by other tasks and timers. This led similar to the backlit for the display or any other device which can be controlled by the timeout feature. We have other functions available also. X timer change period can change the period of the timer at any point this is to delete the timer reset is to reset the timer but x timer start can also be used as the reset if the timer is running. Just like we are doing here whenever the button is pressed, and the timer is still running. This will reset the timer and it will start from the beginning.

www.ingramcontent.com/pod-product-compliance
Lightning Source LLC
LaVergne TN
LVHW051437050326
832903LV00030BD/3138